Pierre Bourdieu's work on culture and practice has made a seminal contribution to the development of the fields of sociology, anthropology and cultural studies over the last fifty years. The interest of Bourdieu (1930–2002) in understanding how and why people act in the world was shared by many of his French counterparts including Gaston Bachelard, Michel de Certeau, Michel Foucault and Henri Lefebvre. However, his empirically based work, which involved the use of photography, observations, questionnaires and interviews to explore the real world, provides a refreshing foil to the rhetorical excesses of his philosopher contemporaries.

Although Pierre Bourdieu's work is little known in the field of architecture, much of his research focuses on understanding how notions of culture are constructed, how culture circulates as 'capital' in societies and how this 'cultural capital' is used by dominant groups to maintain their positions of power.

This short survey introduces readers to Pierre Bourdieu's work on spatial and material culture with the aim of helping architects to understand the social, political, cultural and professional milieu in which they operate.

Helena Webster is a Reader in Architecture at the Department of Architecture, Oxford Brookes University, United Kingdom.

Thinkers for Architects

Series Editor: Adam Sharr, Cardiff University, UK

Editorial board

Jonathan A. Hale, University of Nottingham, UK

Hilde Heynen, KU Leuven, Netherlands

David Leatherbarrow, University of Pennsylvania, USA

Architects have often looked to philosophers and theorists from beyond the discipline for design inspiration or in search of a critical framework for practice. This original series offers quick, clear introductions to key thinkers who have written about architecture and whose work can yield insights for designers.

Deleuze and Guattari for Architects

Andrew Ballantyne

Heidegger for Architects

Adam Sharr

Irigaray for Architects

Peg Rawes

Bhabha for Architects

Felipe Hernández

Merleau-Ponty for Architects

Jonathan Hale

Bourdieu for Architects

Helena Webster

Benjamin for Architects

Brian Elliott

Bourdieu

---

for

Architects

Helena Webster

LONDON AND NEW YORK

First published 2011
by Routledge
2 Park Square, Milton Park, Abingdon, Oxon, OX14 4RN

Simultaneously published in the USA and Canada
by Routledge
270 Madison Avenue, New York, NY 10016

Routledge is an imprint of the Taylor & Francis Group, an informa business

Typeset in Frutiger and Galliard by Wearset Ltd, Boldon, Tyne and Wear
Printed and bound in Great Britain by TJ International Ltd, Padstow, Cornwall

British Library Cataloguing in Publication Data
A catalogue record for this book is available from the British Library

Library of Congress Cataloging-in-Publication Data
Webster, Helena.
Bourdieu for architects / Helena Webster.
p. cm. – (Thinkers for architects)
Includes bibliographical references and index.
1. Bourdieu, Pierre, 1930–2002. 2. Architecture–Philosophy. I. Title.
HM479.B68W435 2011
720.1–dc22

                                    2010003530

ISBN10: 0-415-49614-4 (hbk)
ISBN10: 0-415-49615-2 (pbk)

ISBN13: 978-0-415-49614-8 (hbk)
ISBN13: 978-0-415-49615-5 (pbk)

For Judith, Carol and Charles

Contents

Illustration Credits

1 Chronology: selected publications, biography and events, page 4.

2 Algerian women in traditional dress engaging with imported French fashion, page 14. Pierre Bourdieu, *Untitled*, n.d. R 11, Archive Pierre Bourdieu, Images from Algeria, 1958–61. © Pierre Bourdieu/Fondation Pierre Bourdieu, Saint-Gallen. Courtesy Camera Austria, Graz.

3 A Kabyle house burnt out by the French army during the 'uprooting', page 17. Pierre Bourdieu, *Aïn Aghbel, Collo*, n.d. N 88/786, Archive Pierre Bourdieu, Images from Algeria, 1958–61. © Pierre Bourdieu/Fondation Pierre Bourdieu, Saint-Gallen. Courtesy Camera Austria, Graz.

4 A resettlement camp for mountain tribes in Aïn Aghbel, Collo, page 19. Pierre Bourdieu, *Aïn Aghbel, Collo*, n.d. O 87/780, Archive Pierre Bourdieu, Images from Algeria, 1958–61. © Pierre Bourdieu/Fondation Pierre Bourdieu, Saint-Gallen. Courtesy Camera Austria, Graz.

5 Pierre Bourdieu's annotated field sketch of a Kabyle house plan, page 23. Pierre Bourdieu, Floor Plan of a Kabyle House; manuscript P. Bourdieu, fiches d'Algérie/Collection of Notes from Algeria, n.d. Archive Pierre Bourdieu, Images from Algeria, 1958–61. © Pierre Bourdieu/Fondation Pierre Bourdieu, Saint-Gallen. Courtesy Camera Austria, Graz.

6 The Kabyle house plan, after the diagram of the same name in *Logic of Practice* (Bourdieu, 1990c: 272), page 25. © Éditions de Minuit.

7 The space of social positions/the space of lifestyles, after the diagram of the same name in *Distinction* (Bourdieu, 1984a: 128–9), pages 46–47. © Taylor and Francis/Éditions de Minuit.

8 Variants of the dominant taste: the space of properties and the space of individuals, after the diagram of the same name in *Distinction* (Bourdieu, 1984a: 262), page 50. © Taylor and Francis/Éditions de Minuit.

9 The Paris of *Sentimental Education*, after the map of the same name in *Les règles de l'art* [Bourdieu, 1992], page 95. © Estate of Pierre Bourdieu.

10   The field of cultural production in the field of power and in social space, after the diagram of the same name in *Les règles de l'art* [Bourdieu, 1992], page 97. © Estate of Pierre Bourdieu.

Series Editor's Preface

Adam Sharr

Architects have often looked to thinkers in philosophy and theory for design ideas, or in search of a critical framework for practice. Yet architects and students of architecture can struggle to navigate thinkers' writings. It can be daunting to approach original texts with little appreciation of their contexts. And existing introductions seldom explore architectural material in any detail. This original series offers clear, quick and accurate introductions to key thinkers who have written about architecture. Each book summarises what a thinker has to offer for architects. It locates their architectural thinking in the body of their work, introduces significant books and essays, helps decode terms and provides quick reference for further reading. If you find philosophical and theoretical writing about architecture difficult, or just don't know where to begin, this series will be indispensable.

Books in the *Thinkers for Architects* series come out of architecture. They pursue architectural modes of understanding, aiming to introduce a thinker to an architectural audience. Each thinker has a unique and distinctive *ethos*, and the structure of each book derives from the character at its focus. The thinkers explored are prodigious writers and any short introduction can only address a fraction of their work. Each author – an architect or an architectural critic – has focused on a selection of a thinker's writings which they judge most relevant to designers and interpreters of architecture. Inevitably, much will be left out. These books will be the first point of reference, rather than the last word, about a particular thinker for architects. It is hoped that they will encourage you to read further, offering an incentive to delve deeper into the original writings of a particular thinker.

The *Thinkers for Architects* series has proved highly successful, expanding now to seven volumes dealing with familiar cultural figures whose writings have influenced architectural designers, critics and commentators in distinctive and important ways. Books explore the work of: Gilles Deleuze and Felix Guattari; Martin Heidegger; Luce Irigaray; Homi Bhabha; Maurice Merleau-Ponty; Walter Benjamin; and Pierre Bourdieu. The series continues to expand, addressing an increasingly rich diversity of contemporary thinkers who have something to say to architects.

Adam Sharr is Senior Lecturer at the Welsh School of Architecture, Cardiff University, Principal of Adam Sharr Architects and Editor (with Richard Weston) of *arq: Architectural Research Quarterly* published by Cambridge University Press. He is author of *Heidegger's Hut* (MIT Press, 2006) and *Heidegger for Architects* (Routledge, 2007), also joint editor of *Quality out of Control: Standards for Measuring Architecture* (Routledge, 2010) and *Primitive: Original Matters in Architecture* (Routledge, 2006).

CHAPTER 1

Introduction

This book introduces readers to Pierre Bourdieu's work on spatial and material culture with the aim of helping architects to understand the social, political, cultural and professional milieu in which it operates. The text selects elements of Bourdieu's extensive writings with the aim of stimulating interest in, and providing a method for, a critical examination of the field of architecture.

Although Bourdieu is widely recognised as one of the leading twentieth-century sociologists and a fore-father of the academic discipline of cultural studies, arguably the significance of his work for architects and architecture has not yet been fully acknowledged. Readers may be familiar with Bourdieu's most influential concepts, particularly 'habitus' and 'cultural capital', but few will be conversant with his complete intellectual output. Therefore, this chapter begins by presenting a case for why architects, and others involved in the field of architecture, should engage with Bourdieu's ideas.

Some readers may be familiar with of Bourdieu's more influential concepts, particularly '*habitus*' and 'cultural capital', but few will be conversant with his complete intellectual output.

Bourdieu for architects

Architects talk and write a great deal about architecture; what it is, what makes it 'good', why society needs it, and how it is created. One might argue that the critical discourse within the field of architecture is in a thoroughly healthy state. So, why is there a need for a book that encourages architects to look at the work of Pierre Bourdieu, a thinker from 'outside' the discipline of architecture?

Students spend a long period of learning to 'become' architects through a gradual process of imbibing of the tacit knowledge, beliefs and values of the discipline and, for most, this proves to be a thoroughly fascinating, enjoyable and all-consuming experience. However, one of the results of this process of socialisation and acculturation is that architects come to see the world refracted, or interpreted, through an architectural lens and as a consequence they often become frustrated and intolerant of outsiders (the general public, builders, quantity surveyors, politicians, etc.) who see the world differently. Bourdieu's ideas can help architects to understand this complex phenomenon. He proposes that social groups (what he terms 'fields') within society construct their own particular beliefs and values as a means of reinforcing group cohesion and that these groups compete for the power in society to dictate what is legitimate. Thus, Bourdieu offers architects a way of thinking about of the social construction of their own discipline and its relationship to the social world outside architecture. In addition Bourdieu's research explores many more specific themes that architects should find both fascinating and relevant including: the use of space as a means of oppression; the genesis of creative dispositions; the perception of cultural artefacts; the socio-political role of cultural producers. These are just some of the reasons why architects should look at the work of Pierre Bourdieu.

However, anyone who has attempted to understand Bourdieu's writing will acknowledge that it is not an easy task. First, Bourdieu wrote over forty books and hundreds of articles, mostly in French, and it is not immediately obvious which writings architects will find interesting. Second, the style and structure of Bourdieu's writings, particularly from 1970 to 1990, are very complex and as a result they are often difficult to understand. Third, many of the larger books publish the results of empirical studies into French culture and it is not always clear how one might gain from investing time in reading the results. Last, unless one reads everything that Bourdieu wrote it is very difficult to understand the role that each piece of writing plays in the development of his grand project: an explanation of how people act in the world.

This book aims to help the reader overcome these difficulties by both highlighting the areas of Bourdieu's writings that have particular relevance for architects and explaining them in non-specialist language. The second part of this chapter provides the reader with a brief overview of Bourdieu's life and work, with the aim of helping readers to 'locate' Bourdieu both historically and conceptually. The subsequent chapters are broadly chronological, with the aim of demonstrating the development of Bourdieu's ideas over time. The second chapter looks at his early Algerian work on space and power, and the social construction of space. The third chapter explores his studies on the social construction of aesthetics, including the research that resulted in his most famous book, *La distinction*. Chapter 4 charts the development of Bourdieu's theory of cultural practice, while Chapter 5 looks at three studies that applied the theory to specific cases: fashion, art and literature, and housing. The final chapter describes Bourdieu's 'political turn' that occurred in the last decade of his life, during which time he publicly championed the plight of the oppressed and called for intellectuals, including cultural producers, to oppose neo-liberalism.

Situating Pierre Bourdieu

Pierre Bourdieu was born in 1930 and grew up in a small provincial farming community, Denguin near Pau, in south-west France. During this time Bourdieu was socialised into working-class practices, tastes and values. However, unlike his contemporaries, Bourdieu was encouraged by his father to pursue a formal education which, through his success, took him progressively away, both geographically and socially, from his working-class roots. Over the seventy-two years of his life Bourdieu's career followed a successful academic trajectory: moving from schooling in Pau (1941–7) and Paris (1948–51), to attending university in Paris (1951–4); on to teaching in a provincial French university (1961–4), before becoming a Director of Studies at the École pratique des hautes études en sciences sociales in Paris (1964–2001), Director of the Centre

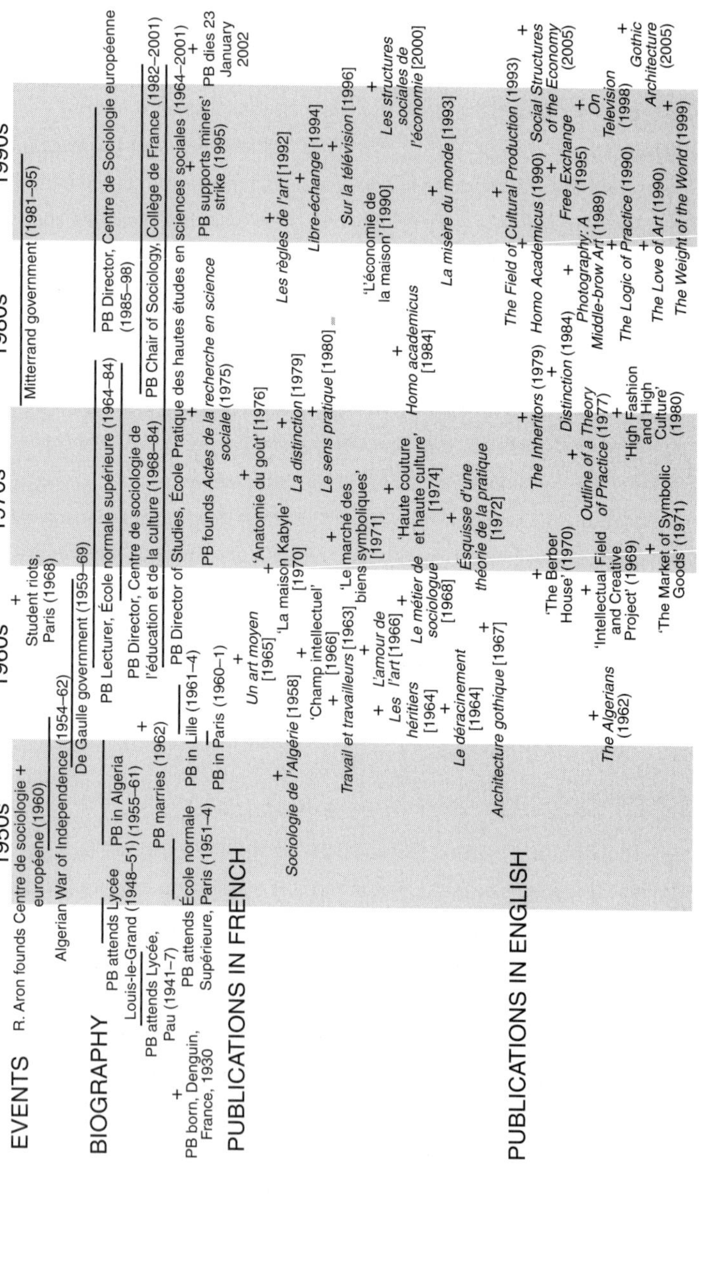

EVENTS

R. Aron founds Centre de sociologie européenne (1960)

Algerian War of Independence (1954–62)

De Gaulle government (1959–69)

Student riots, Paris (1968)

Mitterrand government (1981–95)

BIOGRAPHY

PB born, Denguin, France, 1930

PB attends Lycée Pau (1941–7)

PB attends Lycée Louis-le-Grand (1948–51)

PB attends École normale Supérieure, Paris (1951–4)

PB in Algeria (1955–61)

PB marries (1962)

PB in Lille (1961–4)

PB in Paris (1960–1)

PB Lecturer, École normale supérieure (1964–84)

PB Director, Centre de sociologie de l'éducation et de la culture (1968–84)

PB Director of Studies, École Pratique des hautes études en sciences sociales (1964–2001)

PB founds Actes de la recherche en science sociale (1975)

PB Director, Centre de Sociologie européenne (1985–98)

PB Chair of Sociology, Collège de France (1982–2001)

PB supports miners' strike (1995)

PB dies 23 January 2002

PUBLICATIONS IN FRENCH

Sociologie de l'Algérie [1958]

'Champ intellectuel' [1966]

Travail et travailleurs [1963]

Un art moyen [1965]

'La maison Kabyle' [1970]

'L'amour de l'art' [1966]

Les héritiers [1964]

Le métier de sociologue [1968]

Le déracinement [1964]

Architecture gothique [1967]

'Anatomie du goût' [1976]

La distinction [1979]

Le sens pratique [1980]

'Le marché des biens symboliques' [1971]

'Haute couture et haute culture' [1974]

Esquisse d'une théorie de la pratique [1972]

Homo academicus [1984]

Les règles de l'art [1992]

Libre-échange [1994]

Sur la télévision [1996]

'L'économie de la maison' [1990]

Les structures sociales de l'économie [2000]

La misère du monde [1993]

PUBLICATIONS IN ENGLISH

The Algerians (1962)

'The Berber House' (1970)

'Intellectual Field and Creative Project' (1969)

'The Market of Symbolic Goods' (1971)

The Inheritors (1979)

Outline of a Theory of Practice (1977)

Distinction (1984)

'High Fashion and High Culture' (1980)

The Field of Cultural Production (1993)

Homo Academicus (1990)

Photography: A Middle-brow Art (1989)

The Logic of Practice (1990)

The Love of Art (1990)

Social Structures of the Economy (2005)

Free Exchange (1995)

On Television (1998)

The Weight of the World (1999)

Gothic Architecture (2005)

Figure 1 Chronology: selected publications, biography and events.

de sociologie de l'éducation et de la culture (1968–84), and being elected to the prestigious Collège de France in 1982.

When reflecting back on his own career Bourdieu suggested that his own status as a (peasant) 'outsider' located 'inside' the French educational establishment provided him with a motive (derived from a sense of being discriminated against) and means (the detached objectivity of the outsider) to expose the way that economic, social and especially cultural capital circulated in society and the role that capital played in guiding individual practice and in maintaining and reproducing social hierarchies: 'In France, to come from a distant province … gives you a sort of objective and subjective externality and puts you in a particular relation to the central institutions of French society' (Bourdieu and Wacquant, 1992a: 209). Bourdieu pursued this meta-project throughout his career through a series of anthropological, then historical and sociological studies, many of which were culturally orientated. The form and focus of these studies were inextricably linked to the changes in France's social, political and intellectual context through the mid- to late twentieth century.

Bourdieu studied philosophy, then considered the most prestigious subject in French academic circles, whilst attending the elite École normale supérieure in Paris (1951–4), as a precursor for an assumed academic career in the humanities. However, Bourdieu became increasingly dissatisfied with the apparent disconnection between contemporary French philosophical discourse, led by Jean-Paul Sartre, and his perceptions of the realities of everyday life. In reaction he turned to the up-and-coming 'scientific' discipline of anthropology and particularly to the work of the emerging structural anthropologist Claude Lévi-Strauss for a more convincing theoretical paradigm. Thus, during the 1950s Bourdieu recast himself as a self-taught, empirically orientated, anthropologist and during a period of military service in Algeria he carried out a number of anthropological investigations into the spacio-cultural effects of French colonialisation on the indigenous Kabyle tribes. These studies resulted in a number of publications, including the *Sociologie de l'Algérie* (*Sociology of Algeria*) in 1958 [1958] (1962b) and the seminal *Esquisse d'une théorie de la pratique* (*Outline of a Theory of Practice*) in 1972 [1972a] (1977a). This latter work set out a theory of action and became very influential in the field of anthropology because it exposed a fundamental weakness in the structuralist approach to understanding individual practice (structuralism is the theory that societies are characterised by deep mental structures that determine the actions of individuals), that of mistaking the researcher's perception of practice for practice itself, and pointed to a new 'scientific' approach that later came to be known as 'reflexive' sociology (sociological investigation in which the researcher is aware of their contribution to the construction of meanings throughout the research process). The book also provided a tentative theoretical hypothesis that explained the mutually constituting nature of individual practice and cultural context, an explanation that overcame the deficiencies of both contemporary structuralist accounts, which implied an overwhelming social determinism, and phenomenological accounts, which insisted on the unrestrained freedom of the individual (phenomenology is the theory that reality is no more than individual human experience).

When Bourdieu moved back to France in 1960 he took up university teaching positions in Paris (1960–1) and then in Lille (1961–4). On moving back to Paris in 1964 he joined researchers at Raymond Aron's newly formed Centre for European Sociology in Paris. Here he continued the development of his theory of action and 'scientific' research method through a reworking of his Algerian fieldwork and launched a number of large empirical studies on various aspects of post-war French culture. These were intended to expose any 'hidden' social and cultural systems that might frustrate the achievement of France's post-war aspirations for progressive modernisation. The results of these studies were subsequently published as: *Les héritiers* (*The Inheritors*) [Bourdieu and Passeron, 1964] (Bourdieu and Passeron, 1979), a study of the cultural preferences of French students; *L'amour de l'art* (*The Love of Art*) [Bourdieu, Darbel, and Schnapper, 1966] (Bourdieu, Darbel and Schnapper, 1990), a study of museum attendance; *Un art moyen* (*Photography: A Middle-brow Art*) [Bourdieu, Boltanski, Castel *et al*., 1965] (Bourdieu, Boltanski, Castel *et al*., 1989), a study of photographic practices; and *La reproduction: Eléments pour une théorie du système d'enseignement* (*Reproduction in Education, Society and Culture*) [Bourdieu and Passeron, 1970] (Bourdieu and Passeron, 1977), a theoretical explication of the French education system. Bourdieu used the findings of these studies to support his controversial thesis that 'culture' was an arbitrarily constructed notion, that is, that social groups constructed their own particular temporally contingent notions of 'culture'. Additionally, Bourdieu claimed that his studies demonstrated *par exemple* the mechanisms by which the ruling classes used their particular definitions of culture as part of the armoury of mechanisms through which they established, maintained and reproduced their ruling position.

Bourdieu used the findings of these studies to support his controversial thesis that 'culture' was an arbitrarily constructed notion, that is, that social groups constructed their own particular temporally contingent notions of 'culture'.

This body of work drew on a number of theoretical sources for direction. For instance, Gaston Bachelard's work on the history and philosophy of science (2006) informed Bourdieu's 'scientific' methodology, Max Weber's work on the characteristics of nineteenth-century Protestant Calvinism (2001) informed his understanding of the power of symbolic constructions, and Marxist theory provided the starting point for his notion that society was fuelled by struggles to accumulate capital.

In the following decade Bourdieu went on to elaborate his theoretical ideas in *La distinction: critique sociale du jugement (Distinction: A Social Critique of the Judgement of Taste)* [1979b] (1984a) which is arguably his best-known text. *La distinction* explored the cultural preferences of the French public and at the time of publication the study shocked the French middle classes into recognising that they were complicit in supporting a society which used culture as a mechanism to maintain social hierarchies. In effect *La distinction* and Bourdieu's subsequent work elaborated the theoretical (theory of practice) and methodological (reflexive sociology) notions that had come to fruition in the late 1960s [Bourdieu, Chamboredon and Passeron, 1968] and early 1970s [1972a], although his concern gradually shifted away from a focus on individual practice towards a preoccupation with the internal dynamics of fields of practice and their interrelationship. Within Bourdieu's vast oeuvre there were three studies of culture which were particularly important; *Homo academicus (Homo Academicus)* [1984c] (1990b) included an analysis of the French academic field at the end of the 1960s; *Les règles de l'art (The Rules of Art)* [1992] (1996a) provided a historical study of the socio-genesis of the development of an autonomous cultural field in Paris in the second half of the nineteenth century (focusing particularly on Flaubert); and the little-known *Les structures sociales de l'économie (The Social Structures of the Economy)* [2000a] (2005a) looked at the contingencies that resulted in the increased privatisation of the French housing provision in the 1990s. Alongside these studies Bourdieu produced a number of theoretical texts that expanded, but did not substantially change, his early theoretical notions, including *Le sens pratique (The Logic of Practice)* [1980c] (1990c), which reworked the earlier *Esquisse d'une théorie de la pratique* [1972a] (1977a), and *Méditations pascaliennes (Pascalian Meditations)* [1997] (1999), which contained a detailed critique of the intellectual field and the notion of scholarly reason.

Although Bourdieu's academic work was implicitly motivated by a leftist agenda, through its focus on exposing the 'hidden' mechanisms through which the least privileged in society were oppressed, he did not explicitly engage with the world of politics until the last decade of his life. In the early 1990s Bourdieu began to use his own social and cultural capital as a leading French sociologist for direct political effect by publicly calling on intellectuals to join together and to collaborate with other progressive groups to fight the negative effects of neo-liberalism and globalisation. During the 1990s his new *modus operandi* included; attending demonstrations, speaking at rallies and in the broadcasting media (1998b) (Bourdieu, Poupeau and Discepolo, 2008), forming the radical journal *Liber*, the publication house Raisons d'agir and several international and European intellectual collectives.

In the early 1990s Bourdieu began to use his own social and cultural capital as a leading French sociologist for direct political effect.

During this period he also published several books of a polemical nature including: *La misère du monde* (*The Weight of the World*) [Bourdieu and Accardo, 1993] (Bourdieu and Accardo, 1999), which demonstrated, through a series of intimate case studies, the negative effects of globalisation, and *Sur la télévision* (*On Television*) [1996b] (1998d), which made a critique of the commercialisation of the media. Collectively Bourdieu's last productions communicated the urgency of his concern about the increasing grip of neo-liberalism and the consequential demise of post-war humanist values.

Bourdieu, who died of cancer in 2002, established a reputation as one of the most influential sociologists on the world stage. Despite the fact that Bourdieu's research was deeply connected to its French context, his trans-national contribution included a new research methodology (reflexive sociology) that facilitated research into the situated nature of individual and collective practice, and the production of a theoretical account of practice that accounted for the relationship between the specificity of social contexts and individual practice. Unlike his philosopher contemporaries, such as Michel Foucault, Michel de Certeau and Jacques Derrida, Bourdieu was first and foremost an empirical researcher, who both developed and constantly refined his theoretical concepts in response to the findings of his anthropological, historical and sociological studies. As a consequence Bourdieu always presented his theoretical concepts as working hypotheses and unremittingly encouraged others to undertake further empirical research in other contexts that would test and elaborate his ideas.

CHAPTER 2

The Social Construction of Space

While much of Bourdieu's research focused on decoding the complex class dynamics at work in cultures of late modernity, using France as an exemplar, he spent the early part of his career (1955–1960) in Algeria observing the ways in which French colonialisation was eroding the indigenous culture. In an attempt to understand what was happening Bourdieu rejected the modes of philosophical reasoning that had dominated his university education and turned to methods of anthropological exploration and explanation. During the late 1950s Bourdieu carried out extensive ethnographic fieldwork, including observation, interviews and photography, which provided the basis for a series of articles and books that attempted to provide a corrective to the prevalent French understanding, both from the right and left, of the Algerian situation, and to empower the Algerians by providing them with a deeper understanding of their own cultural heritage.

Bourdieu rejected the modes of philosophical reasoning that had dominated his university education and turned to methods of anthropological exploration and explanation.

These publications contained some of Bourdieu's most explicitly architectural themes. They looked variously at: the cultural destabilisation produced by the displacement of mountain communities to French-designed resettlement camps [Bourdieu and Sayad, 1964a]; the 'cultural limbo' that followed the movement of rural communities to the cities [Bourdieu, Darbel et al., 1963]; and the symbolic content of the Kabyle house [Bourdieu, 1960a] (Bourdieu, 1965: 191–241). Together, this body of work tackled many themes that were subsequently taken up by the late-twentieth-century disciplines of cultural studies, post-colonial studies and cultural geography.

During this period Bourdieu also began the development of a new research methodology that he would subsequently call 'reflexive sociology' and laid the foundations for his seminal 'theory of practice' [1972a] [1980c] that discredited the then structuralist orientation of anthropology.

Bourdieu in Algeria

In 1954 Bourdieu completed his formal education at the École normale supérieure, Paris, as a top graduate and, after gaining an *agrégé de philosophie* (the French certification for university teaching), his trajectory was towards an academic career, teaching and writing philosophy. However, after a short period of teaching at a *lycée* in Moulins (1954–5), Bourdieu, then twenty-five, was conscripted to serve in the French army, first in Versailles and subsequently in Algeria (1955–8). In October 1955 he was assigned to an airbase in the Chellif Valley, 150 km west of the city of Algiers and in 1956 he was reassigned to Algiers where he worked for the French colonial government's Documentation and Information Service.

The young Bourdieu entered Algeria at a time of civil unrest. France's colonisation of Algeria, which had begun in 1830, was the longest and most destructive in the whole of North Africa. During this period the French government pursued policies intended to modernise the country that systematically destroyed the indigenous culture and traditional ways of life. Despite repeated efforts by the Algerians to expel the French, they did not leave until July 1962 following the bloody, eight-year War of Independence.

Bourdieu's direct observations of the negative effects of French colonialism on the Algerian people prompted him to make a political analysis of the situation that challenged the dominant understanding in France (both from the left and from the right). Bourdieu used his time working for the government in Algiers to read extensively in their well-stocked library, including the work of Edmund Husserl, Claude Lévi-Strauss and Georges Ganguilhem, to make observations in the field, and to meet Algerian researchers, including Émile Dermenghem and André Nouschi, whose tacit use of ethnography provided Bourdieu with much of his ethnographic data (Yacine, 2004: 491). During this period Bourdieu progressively abandoned his philosophical allegiances and became committed to socio-ethnography, which he believed better equipped him, as he later put it, 'to write a book of social service' (Yacine, 2004: 494). Bourdieu published the findings of his Algerian research in his first book, *Sociologie de l'Algérie* (*The Algerians*) [1958] (1962b). He later recounted that he wanted the book to highlight 'the plight of the Algerian people and also that of the French settlers whose situation was no less dramatic, whatever else had to be said about their racism' (Bourdieu, 1986: 38) and to 'tell the French, and especially the people on the left, what was really going on in the country of which they knew nothing' (Bourdieu, 2007a: 39).

Drawing on the political writings of Max Weber and Karl Marx, Bourdieu cast the situation as no less than the clash between the logic of a capitalist society, based on the notion of capital accumulation and that of a pre-capitalist society, based on the notion of a 'good-faith economy'.

The first chapters of *Sociologie de l'Algérie* contained straightforward descriptions of the indigenous tribes of Algeria including their demographic distribution and social and economic structures. However, the last chapter, 'The Revolution within the Revolution', provided a critical account of how colonial oppression was leading to the disenchantment of the tribespeople as their traditional culture, social organisations and means of production were being systematically destroyed by the colonial government's policies. Drawing on the political writings of Max Weber and Karl Marx, Bourdieu cast the situation as no less than the clash between the logic of a capitalist society, based on the notion of capital accumulation, and that of a pre-capitalist society based on the notion of a 'good-faith economy'. The book ended with a heroic, if rather emotive, call for revolution:

> A society that has been so greatly revolutionised demands that revolutionary solutions be devised to meet its problems ... Algeria contains such explosive forces that it could well be that there now remains only a choice between chaos and an original form of socialism that will have been carefully designed to meet the needs of the actual situation (1962b: 191–2).

While this passage demonstrates that Bourdieu's political sympathies were clearly aligned with the oppressed Algerians, he refuted their characterisation by French Marxist intellectuals of the time as 'revolutionary peasants'. Rather, Bourdieu cast the Algerians as victims who took to arms, not because they were ideologically motivated, but because they could no longer tolerate colonial oppression and persecution. Yet Bourdieu went on to provide the Algerians with detailed knowledge about their pre-colonial culture that he believed could assist them in the conscious ideological construction of an authentic post-colonial Algeria.

Following the end of Bourdieu's military service in 1958 he chose to stay in Algeria rather than return to Paris, even though the Franco-Algerian war (the Algerian War of Independence) was raging and liberals were susceptible to arrest and torture by the army. He subsequently took up a position as an assistant professor teaching philosophy and sociology in the Faculty of Arts at the University of Algeria. This position allowed Bourdieu to continue his writing on the upheaval of Algerian culture [1959a] [1959b] [1960b] and to participate in two large commissioned field studies. The first project studied the emerging patterns of labour in the city, resulting in the book *Travail et travailleurs en Algérie* (Work and Workers of Algeria) [Bourdieu, Darbel *et al.*, 1963]. The second project studied the social effects caused by the forced expulsion of the indigenous mountain tribes to resettlement camps, and was subsequently published as *Le déracinement: La crise de l'agriculture traditionnelle en Algérie* (The Uprooting: The Crisis of Traditional Agriculture in Algeria) [Bourdieu and Sayad, 1964a].

The study explored the effects of the increasing migration of workers from the countryside to the cities ...

Travail et travailleurs en Algérie, which was later reworked as 'The Disenchantment of the World' and published as one of three essays in *Algérie soixante* [1977b] (1979a: 1–94), drew on extensive ethnographic fieldwork (questionnaires, interviews, photographs and observations) that were carried out between 1958 and 1961 by a team that included Bourdieu, from the Algerian branch of the French National Institute of Statistics and Economic Studies (INSEE) (Bourdieu, 2004c: 423). The study explored the effects of the increasing migration of workers from the countryside to the cities and was undertaken at the request of ARDES (the Association for Demographic Economic and Society Research) and financed by the Algerian Development Fund. The study found that migrants were experiencing profound 'disenchantment' as a result of being

Figure 2 Algerian women in traditional dress engaging with imported French fashion.

compelled by the colonial government's modernisation of land ownership and agrarian production to move from the familiar environment of the countryside, with its economy underpinned by the notions of exchange, gift and honour, to the alien environment of the cities, with its market economy, in search of paid work.

The study identified a growing number of migrants, a sub-proletariat, who were effectively condemned to a life of economic misery in the burgeoning city slums. However, instead of reinforcing the common perception of the slums as dirty, ugly and disorganised, Bourdieu presented them as places

> for a very complex life, for a real economy with an inherent logic, where you see a great deal of resourcefulness, an economy that at least offers a lot of people a minimum with which to survive and, above all, for social survival – i.e. to escape the shame for a self respecting man of doing nothing and contributing nothing to his family's livelihood (Bourdieu, 2007b: 26).

Yet, while identifying an optimistic 'economy of poverty' or 'economy of the slums' (2007b: 26), in much the same way Mike Davis did some forty years later (1996), Bourdieu also presented the new urban sub-proletariat as being psychologically lost; as 'floating between two cultures' (Wacquant, 2004: 390).

Bourdieu presented the new urban sub-proletariat as psychologically lost; as 'floating between two cultures'.

While the first part of *Travail et travailleurs en Algérie* presented the results of the team's research, the second part, written by Bourdieu alone, offered an analysis of the results together with a series of supporting photographs. The well-observed photographs poignantly captured the material and spatial dimensions of a people 'floating between two cultures' (see Figure 2). Bourdieu started taking photographs in Algeria when his military service ended and he subsequently took over 1,200 photographs. These photographs were only recovered from his house in the Pyrenees in 1999 and were subsequently archived at Camera Austria in Graz [2003b]. In a later reflective discussion with Franz Schultheis, Bourdieu talked about his photographs as having two functions: a documentary function, 'to remember something, later to be able to describe it'; and a more searching 'way of looking ... it was a way of sharpening my gaze, of looking more closely at something, of finding a way into the subject' (Schultheis, 2007: 24). Bourdieu's photographs explored the notion of inhabitation and particularly the interrelation between the social, cultural, spatial and material rather the aesthetic dimension of architectural form. For instance, as part of the fieldwork for *Travail et travailleurs en Algérie,* Bourdieu took photographs of the stalls (architecture with a small 'a') created by hawkers and street vendors that demonstrated their ability to invent new 'honourable' professions and to ingeniously evoke the qualities of 'real' shop windows (Schultheis, 2007: 26). Bourdieu also took a series of poignant photographs in Blida, a commercial town located 50 km to the south-east of Algiers, that captured the cultural dichotomies of the time through jarring juxtapositions of French and Algerian dress, street signs, commerce and everyday objects (Bourdieu, 2003c: 176–202).

Travail et travailleurs en Algérie concluded with a description of the way rural migrants experienced their new modern city housing as impoverished and paradoxically, constraining domestic environments, despite the improved space standards, facilities and services (Bourdieu, 1979a: 75–91). Bourdieu's findings suggested that the new form of housing disrupted the operation of the tribal family structure and the traditional relationship between work and living. He also found that living in the city also placed new financial demands on the inhabitants in the form of rent, gas, electricity and furniture. Bourdieu described the city apartments as 'a system of demands inscribed in objective space and asking to be fulfilled, a universe strewn with expectations and thereby generating needs and dispositions' (1979a: 85). That is, having been made for the 'modern man, the apartment demands the behaviour of a modern man' (1979a: 86), and not for those used to agrarian ways of life. While Bourdieu's analysis post-dated Friedrich Engels' 1845 anti-capitalist tract on working-class housing (2009), which claimed that housing was a mechanism of social control, it notably predated Henri Lefebvre's *The Social Production of Space* (1991), which developed a general theory of the relationship between power and space, by some ten years.

... having been made for the 'modern man, the apartment demands the behaviour of a modern man' ...

Le déracinement [Bourdieu and Sayad, 1964a] was based on a study of the colonial government's policy to forcibly displace the mountain communities in the north of Algeria, the Berbers, to resettlement camps. The government saw the resettlement plan as a means of destroying the strongholds of the National Liberation Front guerrillas and their actions resulted in the resettlement of a

Figure 3 A Kabyle house burnt out by the French army during the 'uprooting'.

quarter of the Algerian population by 1960 (2004c: 445–6). The research for this second study was also undertaken at the request of the Association for Demographic Economic and Society Research (ARDES) and was financed by the Algerian Development Fund. The fieldwork was carried out between 1959 and 1960 by Bourdieu in conjunction with Abdelmalek Sayad, an Algerian researcher from the Kabyle tribe (a Berber tribe from the Kabylia region). It involved extensive interviews with the inhabitants of the resettlement camps as well as dangerous expeditions into the 'forbidden zones' of the Atlas Mountains to make notes and photographic records of mountain houses and villages that had been destroyed by the French army (see Figure 3).

The text provided poignant descriptions of both the systematic destruction of the mountain villages and the ways in which the location, form and operation of the resettlement camps disrupted the traditional Berber way of life. For instance, it described how the camps were often surrounded by walls or barbed wire and how the stables and storerooms were placed with the guardrooms in the boundary walls rather than in the individual houses, which together created a new physical divide between home and work (see Figure 4). The text also described the way that the militaristic, regimented layout of the camp at Djebabra frustrated the ability of previously dispersed Berber families to physically express their group identities (Bourdieu and Sayad, 1964a: 72–5), and how the camp at Kerkera, that housed 113 families, was located in the middle of a swampy plain with no land or equipment available for cultivation or livestock grazing and thus denied the residents any possibility of a livelihood (Bourdieu and Sayad, 1964a: 59–67).

The text concluded by describing how the forced transformations in settlement patterns and domestic space had irreversible destructive effects on Berber culture:

> It was if the colonisers had instinctively discovered the anthropological law which states that the structure of habitat is the symbolic projection of the most fundamental structures of culture; to reorganise it is to provoke a general transformation of the whole cultural system itself (Bourdieu and Sayad, 1964a: 26).

Figure 4 A resettlement camp for mountain tribes in Aïn Aghbel, Collo.

Although the text for *Le déracinement* was completed in 1962, perhaps not surprisingly, the Algerian Development Agency delayed its publication by two years due to the perceived political sensitivity of its contents.

In the tradition of a Marxist narrative Bourdieu argued that ... the colonial government knowingly introduced 'disruptions' into Algerian life as a means to ensure their hold on power and further their economic interests.

Travail et travailleurs en Algérie and *Le déracinement* were more than mere documentary records of events. Bourdieu later described that he had 'wanted to work out the logic and trans-historical effects of these sweeping compulsory resettlements of the population' (2007b: 27). Thus, in the tradition of a Marxist narrative Bourdieu argued that his fieldwork provided empirical evidence that supported his hypothesis that the colonial government knowingly introduced 'disruptions' into Algerian life as a means to ensure their hold on power and further their economic interests.

Bourdieu on Algeria – structural anthropology and beyond

Bourdieu's time in Algeria came to an abrupt end when, in May 1961, he was advised by the military to leave to avoid the risk of assassination. Bourdieu's friendships and writings [Bourdieu, 1959a, 1959b, 1960b] had resulted in the far right regarding him as a dangerous troublemaker and, after the rightwing Algiers *putsch* in April 1961, his name was on a list compiled by advocates of 'Algérie française' of people to be eliminated. Fortuitously, Raymond Aron, a leading French sociologist, who had noticed Bourdieu during a trip to Algiers as president of the baccalaureate jury for Algeria and Tunisia, facilitated Bourdieu's immediate transfer to the Faculty of Arts at the University of Sorbonne, Paris. In the following year Bourdieu moved to a teaching post at the University of Lille. However, during his year in Paris Bourdieu re-read Marx, and attended seminars by the structural anthropologist Claude Lévi-Strauss, who had recently risen to ascendancy in French intellectual circles, at the Collège de France, and ethnology lectures at the Musée de l'Homme (Bourdieu, 1986: 39). These experiences led Bourdieu to re-cast himself as a structural anthropologist/ ethnologist and to use this new theoretical 'lens' to revisit his Algerian fieldwork. Bourdieu thought that structural anthropology might provide the post-colonial Algerians with an insight into the deep structures of their pre-colonial culture and thereby provide the foundations for the building of a new post-colonial Algeria. Subsequently, in *Algérie soixante* [1977b] (1979a) Bourdieu outlined his conception of the political role of the ethnologist in Algeria: 'What one can require in all rigorousness of the ethnologist is that he attempt to restore to other men the meaning of their behaviours, of which the colonial system, among other things, dispossessed them' (Bourdieu, 1979a: ix n.1). Despite the fact that the premise on which structural anthropology was based, that one could access the past from the data of the present, has subsequently been heavily criticised by academics (Goodman, 2003: 786) (Goodman and Silverstein, 2009), at the time Bourdieu's idea of reconstituting the peasant cultures of the past provided a powerful counterpoint to the views of the emerging Algerian elite who saw the destruction of the old culture as a necessary step towards creating a modern post-colonial country.

Bourdieu thought that structural anthropology might provide the post-colonial Algerians with an insight into the deep structures of their pre-colonial culture and thereby provide the foundations for the building of a new post-colonial Algeria.

Although short-lived, Bourdieu's attempt to disclose the deep structures that underpinned pre-colonial Algerian culture produced, amongst other things, perhaps the best-known structuralist study of the house. Bourdieu adopted a Lévi-Straussian paradigm for his seminal study of the Kabyle (or Berber) house. Following Ferdinand de Saussure's (1857–1919) work on the structure of language, Claude Lévi-Strauss argued that cultures subconsciously constructed a shared but 'arbitrary' understanding of their particular worlds as a means to make them intelligible. These constructions were akin to systems that were characterised by hidden semantic structures that connected each discrete part to the whole through a hierarchy of binary oppositions. Lévi-Strauss suggested that these subconscious structures were to be found manifest in the symbolic aspects of culture including language, artefacts, sacred and profane architecture, decoration, art, myths, songs, rituals and, although not readily apparent to participants, could be discerned by the trained eye of the anthropologist. Lévi-Strauss famously illustrated this idea in his structuralist study of food, *The Raw and the Cooked* (1983), in which he suggested that the opposition between raw and cooked food was a direct expression of a more elementary opposition between nature and culture. Further, Lévi-Strauss believed that it was via the symbolic dimensions of life that a culture's history, values and beliefs were received, repeated and learned.

Following Lévi-Strauss's lead, Bourdieu identified the Kabyle house, which was at the centre of Kabyle society, as a prime candidate for a structuralist analysis. Although there had been many previous anthropological descriptions of the Kabyle house, Bourdieu suggested that they were deficient because they failed to account for the existence, or significance, of domestic artefacts or bodily activities (1970a: 152 n.2). For Bourdieu buildings, objects and actions were part of the same symbolic system. Thus, he proceeded to analyse his fieldwork data (photographs, field notes, interview transcripts, etc.), that had been collected in various villages in the mountainous Kabylia region of Algeria and in resettlement camps, through a structuralist lens (1977a: 204 n.54) (see Figure 5).

Bourdieu later recounted that his field data was transcribed on to 1,500 punch cards that recorded specific details about many aspects of Kabyle culture (farming calendars, social groupings, the construction of houses and villages, gender divisions, the organisation of space, marriage rites, agriculture, cooking, woven goods, pottery, sayings, songs, poetry and rites of passage) that were subsequently indexed and analysed to make structural linkages (1990c: 8). Bourdieu first published the results of his analysis in an essay 'La maison kabyle ou le monde renversé' ('The Kabyle House or the world reversed') [1960a]. Another, slightly revised version was subsequently published in a volume of essays that commemorated the sixtieth anniversary of Claude Lévi-Strauss some ten years later [1970b] (1970a). This paper presented a remarkably vivid textual description of an idealised Kabyle house (acting as a synecdoche for Kabyle culture) that, sadly, contained only two illustrations: a diagram of the orientation of the house and a plan of the internal layout.

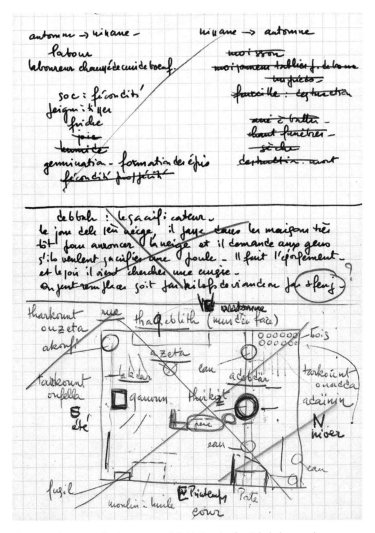

Figure 5 Pierre Bourdieu's annotated field sketch of a Kabyle house plan.

Bourdieu's methodology was subsequently appropriated by many authors to unravel the symbolic dimensions of domestic form and space.

It was this second version of the paper that subsequently gained worldwide recognition from anthropologists, cultural theorists, sociologists and architects and as a result was reprinted many times [1972a: 45–69] (1973a) (2000b) (2003c). Such was the paper's influence that its methodology was appropriated by many authors to unravel the symbolic dimensions of domestic form and space in diverse contexts (Löfgrem, 2003) (Mitchell, 1988: 48–52) (Pellow, 2004) (Robben, 1989). The only way to really appreciate the sophistication of Bourdieu's exegesis is to read the original text [1960a] [1970b] (1970a). However, given its density and lack of structure the following explanation might help by way of an introduction.

The text began with a straightforward description of the house: a modest rectangular structure of undressed stone, with two doors, a single space divided by a low wall into two parts; two thirds for the humans, where a hearth, cooking area and weaving loom were located and the other, slightly lower and darker third, where the animals and the water vessels were located (see Figure 6). Thus far the text was purely descriptive and the objects were represented as merely signalling their functional use.

However, Bourdieu continued by suggesting that the functional role of the house alone could not fully explain its form. He proposed that the beliefs and practices associated with the Kabyle mythico-ritual system, which formed the core ordering principle of society, were a key determinant of the form of the house. It followed, Bourdieu claimed, that the Kabyle house was 'organised according to the same oppositions which govern all the universe' (1970a: 160). Or, as Silverstein commented, Bourdieu presented the house as 'a single, concrete social institution [that] stands in as a synecdoche (part represents whole) for a rooted cultural unity whose existence the ethnologist

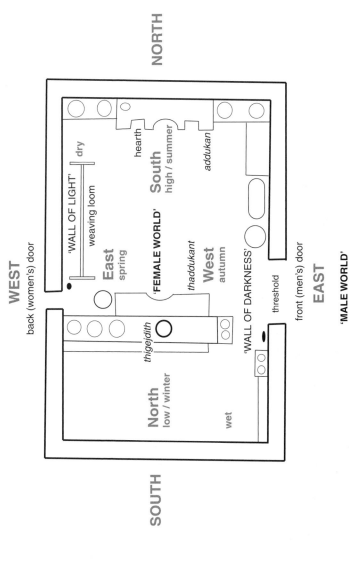

Figure 6 The Kabyle house plan, after the diagram of the same name in *Logic of Practice* (Bourdieu, 1990c: 272).

cannot (or can no longer) observe directly' (Silverstein, 2004: 554). The exegesis that followed attempted to demonstrate the ways in which the Kabyles' strong connection with a mythical natural world, the seasons, the daily cycle, the life cycle, fertility etc., was reflected in the symbolism of various aspects of the house: its orientation, form, structure, layout, artefacts, and its use – although Bourdieu conceded that the Kabyle symbolic system alone could not wholly account or determine the form of the house (1970a: 153 n.5). Additionally, as a structuralist, Bourdieu attempted to demonstrate how symbolic expression always occurred in the form of binary oppositions (male–female, high–low, human–animal, day–night, wet–dry, etc.) and the ways in which individual binary oppositions were connected, through parallels, homologies, metaphors, comparisons and antimonies, via a hierarchical structure, into a complete and balanced system. For example, Bourdieu suggested that the orientation of the house was primarily determined by the Kabyles' cosmological beliefs. Thus, the principal axis of the house was aligned east–west so that the main entrance faced the rising sun. Further, from this elementary opposition there followed a series of homologous secondary oppositions, such as dawn–dusk, spring–autumn, light–dark, men's door–women's door.

Arguably Bourdieu's most ingenious exegesis was his deciphering of the elementary male–female binary oppositions within the house. He suggested, supported by proverbs such as 'Man is the lamp of the outside and woman the lamp of the inside' (1970a: 160), that the Kabyle defined the external world as male and the internal world as female and as a result a male reading of the house would be in binary opposition to a female reading:

> whereas, for the man, the house is less a place one goes into than a place from which one goes out, the woman can only confer upon these two movements and the different definitions of the house which form an integral part with them, an inverse importance and meaning, since movement towards the outside consists above all for her of acts of expulsion and it is her specific role to be responsible for all movement towards the inside, that is to say, from the threshold towards the fireplace (1970a: 165).

Bourdieu's most ingenious exegesis was his deciphering of the elementary male–female binary oppositions within the house.

It followed, Bourdieu suggested, that the east wall from the 'male' outside is necessarily the west wall from the 'female' inside and, likewise, the west wall from the 'male' outside was the east wall from the 'female' inside. Further, he argued that because the west internal wall was bathed with light from the main door in the opposite wall it was termed the 'wall of light' and was associated with dawn, spring, fertility and working the loom. In contrast, the east internal wall was termed the 'wall of darkness' because it was dark against the light of the open main door and was associated with the storage of water, male sleep and the dark end of the house, the stable. Bourdieu argued that the gendered reading of the house could be extended to a dichotomous reading of the gable walls:

> Likewise, the two gable walls, the wall of the stable and the wall of the fireplace, take on two opposed meanings depending on which of their sides is being considered: to the external north corresponds the south (and the summer) of the inside, that is to say, the side of the house which is in front of one and on one's right when one goes in facing the weaving loom; to the external south corresponds the inside north (and the winter), that is to say, the stable, which is situated behind and on the left when one goes from the door towards the fireplace (1970a: 168).

He also revealed a male/female binary opposition in the primary structure of the house:

> at the centre of the dividing wall ... stands the main pillar, supporting the governing beam and all the framework of the house. Now this governing beam which connects the gables and spreads the protection of the male part of the house to the female part (*asalas alemmas*, a masculine term) is

identified explicitly with the master of the house, whilst the main pillar upon which it rests, which is the trunk of a forked tree (*thigejdith*, a feminine term), is identified with the wife (1970a: 156).

Bourdieu concluded his ingenious exegesis of the house's male–female symbolism by suggesting that:

to each exterior side of the wall (*essur*) there corresponds a region of interior space ... which has a symmetrical and inverse sense signification in the system of internal oppositions; each of the two spaces can therefore be defined as the set of movements made to effect the same change of position, that is to say a semi-rotation, in relation to the other, the threshold acting as the axis of rotation (1970a: 168).

In other words, he suggested that the threshold of the house acted as a quasi-magical pivot between the male world and the female world, or the 'male world reversed'.

Bourdieu's text went on to suggest the presence of another symbolic system based on the fundamental binary opposition nature–culture which, he claimed, set up a series of linked binary oppositions in the symbolic layout and uses of the house.

The ingenuity and detail of Bourdieu's exegesis [of the Kabyle house] was undeniably impressive.

For example, he suggested that the nature-versus-culture binary found expression in the north (for animals)/south (for humans) spatial division of the interior and was also evidenced in a series of secondary binary oppositions: low–high; dark–light; flagstone floor – black clay and cow dung floor; storage of wet, moist or raw food – storage of dry food; female sleeping area – male sleeping area; secret natural activities (sex, birth, death, taboo) – open cultured activities (fire, cooking, weaving, receiving guests, honour).

The ingenuity and detail of Bourdieu's exegesis was undeniably impressive. Yet, in the decades following the publication of the essay his analysis was increasingly discredited along with structural anthropology itself. The central criticisms of Bourdieu's analysis were cogently summarised by Richard Jenkins in *Pierre Bourdieu* (2002: 36–39) as: first, that Bourdieu's house could not escape being an 'idealised', ahistorical (i.e. unrelated to history) archetype (i.e. an original model or type) because it was based on the nostalgic memories of a displaced people; second, in Bourdieu's Kabyle society individual people did not really exist except as abstracted subjects whose lives were predetermined by the house form and the culture's rituals; third, Bourdieu's inference that there was never any ambiguity in the meaning of symbols allowed neither room for varied interpretations nor room for dissent (de Certeau's notion that real people operated in the cracks between the rules (de Certeau, 1984) had no place in Bourdieu's categorical model). Finally, critics suggested that Bourdieu's identification of symbolic binary oppositions and their linkages were merely the artistic creations of a western anthropologist's imagination, rather than an exegesis of an authentic structure of meaning.

Coincidentally, in the papers that Bourdieu was writing in parallel to his analysis of the Kabyle house, that included 'The Attitude of the Algerian Peasant towards Time' (1963) and 'Le sentiment de l'honneur dans la société kabyle' ('The Sentiment of Honour in Kabyle Society') [1960a] (1965), it was already evident that he was becoming increasingly disenchanted with the objectivism implicit in the structuralist paradigm. Subsequently, in Bourdieu's *Le sens pratique* (*The Logic of Practice*) [1980c] (1990c), where the analysis of the Kabyle house was reproduced in an appendix (1990c: 271–83), he admitted to the limitations of the study and suggested that his subsequent 'theory of practice' went some way to ameliorate the problems of the structuralist paradigm by inserting both the notion of the active agent (a shift from rule to strategy) and the reflexive anthropologist (the process of objectifying the process of objectification) (1990c: 30–41).

CHAPTER 3

The Anatomy of Taste

Bourdieu's studies of the Kabyle, as discussed in Chapter 2, demonstrated how the 'arbitrary', or constructed, symbolic dimensions of tribal culture, as manifest in objects and practices, both supported and reproduced shared beliefs, meanings and values and thereby maintained social cohesion within individual tribal groups. His 'idealised' study of the Kabyle, or Berber, house [1960a] [1970b] (1970a) provided a *prima facie* example of the way that the material and spatial properties of the house – its orientation, layout, arrangement of furniture – worked in tandem with the daily and seasonal routines and ritual practices of the inhabitants to sustain the shared meanings and structures of Kabyle society. Additionally, in the earlier publication *Sociologie de l'Algérie* [1958] Bourdieu suggested that symbolic objects and practices were used within tribal groups to differentiate between members (Robbins, 1991: 117). He suggested that those group members who possessed objects or carried out activities of value were conferred with 'distinction', or status, by the group. The findings of Bourdieu's slightly later study of the peasant matrimonial 'game', 'Célibat et condition paysanne' [1962a: 49], which was carried out in his home province of Béarn, confirmed the conclusions of his Algerian research. Bourdieu discovered that a Béarnais bachelor's social status was derived as much from his 'symbolic capital', including the numbers of storeys of his house ('great' or 'little' houses) and the social position of his family ('great' or 'little' families) as from his monetary worth, or 'economic capital' [1962a: 48]. The coincidence of Bourdieu's findings in two different contexts, Algeria and Béarn, led him to suggest that his notion of 'symbolic capital' was a fundamental dimension of a general 'theory of practice'.

Bourdieu's 'theory of practice' suggested that all actions, even those understood as disinterested or of no purpose, were to be conceived economically as actions aimed at the maximisation of material or symbolic gain.

This hypothesis was radical in that it challenged the, then dominant, structuralist notion that the symbolic realm was the product of the logic of the human mind and replaced it with a utilitarian model that put symbolic practices on the same level as economic practices, that is, as strategies in the competition for prestige or standing in the social hierarchy. Bourdieu's 'theory of practice' suggested that all actions, even those understood as disinterested or of no purpose, were to be conceived economically as actions aimed at the maximisation of material or symbolic gain (Bourdieu, 1977a: 177–8). Thus, Bourdieu's fieldwork among the Kabyles and Béarnais seeded the idea that symbolic goods and practices played an important role in constructing, sustaining and reproducing the 'arbitrary' values and practices of societies and in acting as markers of social difference. During Bourdieu's tenure at the University of Lille (1961–4) he began the process of testing whether these notions, which had been developed in relation to pre-industrial societies, could be extended to account for practices in highly differentiated industrial societies such as France.

Early studies of French culture

Throughout the 1960s and early 1970s Bourdieu undertook a series of empirical studies that explored the wide-ranging cultural tastes and practices present in French society. These empirical studies provided the groundwork, both methodologically and theoretically, for *La distinction* [1979b] (1984a), Bourdieu's seminal work on the class-based construction of aesthetics and its role in sustaining the interests of the elite classes in society.

On returning to France in 1961 Bourdieu was caught up in the *ethos* of post-war reconstruction in which education was conceived as a key tool for achieving economic, social and cultural renewal. President de Gaulle's egalitarian vision for France included the notion that bringing 'high' culture to the masses would contribute to creating a more educated and therefore a more productive society. To this end de Gaulle instigated numerous projects, from broadening the scope of the French education system to the building of numerous *maisons de culture* throughout France (Grenfell, 2004: 40). In this context it was perhaps not surprising that Bourdieu elected to explore the French education system, initially from his new base in the Faculty of Arts at the University of Lille and then, in 1964, from his position at the Centre for European Sociology in Paris. Bourdieu's first book on education, *Les héritiers: Les étudiants et la culture* (*The Inheritors: French Students and their Relations to Culture*) [Bourdieu and Passeron, 1964] (Bourdieu and Passeron, 1979), published the findings of a large sociological study of the cultural tastes and practices of students attending the University of Lille and several other French provincial universities.

Bourdieu's findings suggested that the university system, its structure, pedagogy and rituals, implicitly ... disadvantaged students from families with a low social status.

The findings of the study, which was based on student responses to questionnaires that explored their recognition of a wide range of cultural forms and practitioners, allowed Bourdieu to correlate artistic competence with socio-economic background. The results of the research suggested that students from privileged families arrived at university with a range of dispositions, including dress sense, deportment and knowledge of art, music and literature, which correlated closely with those of the cultural elite. Further, Bourdieu's findings suggested that the university system, its structure, pedagogy and rituals, implicitly favoured this group of students and disadvantaged students from families with a low social status. At this point in his career Bourdieu's 'solution' to the inequity he found in the education system was the instigation of 'rational pedagogy', a method of learning and teaching that recognised the individuality of each student, as opposed to one that 'favoured the favoured' (Stevens, 2002). Bourdieu believed that 'rational pedagogy' would allow previously excluded classes access to education and thereby to high culture.

In 1964 Bourdieu moved from Lille to Paris to take up a position as Director of Studies at the École pratique des hautes études en sciences sociales and began working with Raymond Aron at the newly formed Centre for European Sociology. In the following years Bourdieu continued to develop his own theory of practice (the interrelation between individual action, the immediate context within which individuals operate, and the position of this context within social space) through a series of theoretical and empirical studies into French cultural practices. In parallel Bourdieu also made a significant contribution to the consolidation of the new disciple of sociology through the development of a 'reflexive' sociological research method (that rejected both formalist and structuralist methodologies), which culminated in the publication of a textbook for social researchers entitled *Le métier de sociologue* (*The Craft of Sociology*) [Bourdieu, Chamboredon and Passeron, 1968] (Bourdieu, Chamboredon and Passeron, 1991). Bourdieu's research projects provided him with a vehicle for the continuous testing and revising of both his hypotheses on the nature of practice and his sociological methodology.

Visiting museums

Three studies from the 1960s, two empirical and one theoretical, were particularly pertinent to Bourdieu's continuing interrogation of the relationship between aesthetics, culture and society. The first study, published in 1966 as *L'amour de l'art: les musées d'art européens et leur public* (*The Love of Art: European Art Museums and Their Public*) [Bourdieu, Darbel, and Schnapper, 1966] (Bourdieu, Darbel, and Schnapper, 1990), investigated the museum-visiting habits of the French public and utilised the quantitative and qualitative research methods previously employed in the research for *Les héritiers*. The study involved asking a sample of people from different social groups a range of questions about their museum-visiting habits: how often they visited museums, what type of museums they preferred, how long they spent on each visit, how long they spent viewing each exhibit, and whether they thought that museums were more like churches or libraries. Not surprisingly perhaps, Bourdieu's findings demonstrated that the most highly educated respondents preferred visiting high-art museums; they visited museums often, they spent a long period of time on each visit and in front of each exhibit, and they perceived museums as being 'like' libraries. In contrast, the findings revealed that the least-educated respondents preferred visiting ethnographic-type museums, they rarely visited museums, their visits and time in front of each exhibit were short, and they thought that museums were 'like' churches. More contentiously, Bourdieu's findings dispelled the commonly held notion that museums were 'open' to all, by presenting evidence that suggested that the very institutional nature of the museums, their structures, rituals and forms, were so alien to the least educated groups in society that they effectively excluded themselves. At this point Bourdieu continued to believe in the emancipating potential of education and, as a result, he insisted that all cultural institutions, such as the universities cited in *Les héritiers*, needed to alter their pedagogic practices so that all groups in society had an equitable access to high culture. Consequentially Bourdieu suggested that museums needed to adapt their access programmes to make it easier for the poorly educated classes to visit and feel comfortable in museums, even though the results of his own study suggested that these types of initiatives only resulted in attracting more middle-class visitors.

Bourdieu's findings dispelled the commonly held notion that museums were 'open' to all, by presenting evidence that suggested that … the least-educated groups in society … effectively excluded themselves.

Bourdieu went on to use these findings to support his general thesis that institutions played an important role in both legitimising high culture (i.e. those forms of culture valued by the cultural elite) and in reproducing high culture in the children of cultural elite.

Bourdieu also used the respondents' answers to questions about their conception and perception of museum artefacts to support his radical hypothesis about the nature of aesthetic appreciation. He argued that the capacity to appreciate art was not a 'gift' but rather a competence, or 'good taste', acquired through education and socialisation that was merely presented as 'natural' by those who possessed it as a means for them to claim superiority over those who lacked competence, that is, those with 'poor' taste (Bourdieu, Darbel and Schnapper, 1990: 1). According to Bourdieu, any aesthetic reading of a painting required the viewer to possess the correct 'codes' to decipher the formal and symbolic aspects of the work which, in his view, were constructed by the cultural elite in specific socio-historical contexts. Bourdieu cited the following research findings in support of his thesis. First, his research found that the most-educated museum visitors spent the longest time in front of individual paintings and artefacts (i.e. they possessed the codes necessary to appreciate the work). Second, he found that the most-educated visitors possessed prior knowledge of artists, periods and styles, whilst those with little education did not (i.e. they could locate the work in relation to other works). Third, the most-educated viewers described the art and artefacts they viewed in terms of their formal properties, their style, technique and meaning in relation to other artefacts, while those with little education described the art and artefacts in functional or literal terms. Bourdieu concluded that only the acculturated had the capacity to decode cultural works and thereby the potential to achieve educational benefit from their museum visits.

A theory of art perception

Bourdieu expanded his thesis on the 'arbitrary' (social construction) of aesthetic perception in a purely theoretical essay, 'Outline of a Sociological Theory of Art Perception' (1968a) [1968b] (Bourdieu and Johnson, 1993: 215–37). This essay both extended the arguments Bourdieu had made in *L'amour de l'art* and provided a complementary text to his earlier theoretical essay on artistic production, 'Champ intellectuel et projet créateur' ('Intellectual Field and the Creative Project') [1966a] (1969) (1971a). In the earlier seminal text he had argued that both artistic production and reception occurred within specific socio-historical settings which defined what was valued and why. In 'Outline of a Sociological Theory of Art Perception' Bourdieu went on to define aesthetic perception as

> **a signifier which signifies nothing other than itself, does not consist of considering it 'without connecting it with anything other than itself, either emotionally or intellectually' ... but rather of noting its distinctive stylistic *features* by relating it to the ensemble of works forming the class to which it belongs, and to these works only (Bourdieu and Johnson, 1993: 222).**

Although Bourdieu's interest in aesthetics was clearly present in much of his contemporary work on Algerian [1960a] (1965) and Béarnais culture (1962a), the publication of 'Outline of a Sociological Theory of Art Perception' reflected a new explicit engagement with the academic literature on aesthetics.

[Bourdieu] argued that both artistic production and reception occurred within specific socio-historical settings which defined what was valued and why.

For instance, the essay made reference to Erwin Panofsky's quasi-scientific notion of three levels of art appreciation which might be summarised as: first, the literal recognition of subject matter and its expressive qualities ('naïve beholders'); second, the recognition of conventional symbols (iconography) as understood at the time of viewing ('educated beholders'); and finally, the recognition that the painting was the result of the artist working strategically within a social context ('art historians') (Panofsky, 1939). Perhaps it was not a coincidence that these three categories of art perception were homologous with the three modes of knowledge, 'subjective', 'objective' and 'reflexive', that Bourdieu outlined some four years later in *Esquisse d'une théorie de la pratique*

[1972a] (1977a). However, in this essay Bourdieu used Panofsky's categories to point to the inevitable misalignment between the artist's intention in creating a work of art and the viewer's asynchronous perception of that work. As he explained:

> **the history of the instruments for the perception of the work is the essential complement of the history of the instruments for the production of the work, to the extent that every work is, so to speak, made twice, by the originator and by the beholder, or rather, by the society to which the beholder belongs (Bourdieu and Johnson, 1993: 224).**

This statement refuted the commonly held tacit belief that the meaning of a work of art was somehow latent in the artefact and it was merely waiting to be 'found' by any viewer equipped with the correct degree of aesthetic competence. Bourdieu proceeded, in a radical politicisation of Panofsky's work, to argue that the form of artistic competence demonstrated by 'educated beholders' (i.e. the ability to decode a broad spectrum of cultural works in accordance with the aesthetic codes of the day) was gained through a combination of a cultivated family upbringing, including a repeated exposure to culture, and schooling, and as a consequence was neither a natural nor a universally distributed capability.

Bourdieu proceeded ... to argue that the form of artistic competence demonstrated by 'educated beholders' ... was gained through a combination of a cultivated family upbringing ... and schooling.

He also argued that artistic competence, as a form of cultural capital, and like other forms of capital, tended to follow unequal patterns of accumulation (Bourdieu and Johnson, 1993: 227–37). Therefore, those who possessed artistic competence had it in their own interests to both define what constituted artistic competence and to restrict who could have access to it. Bourdieu further suggested that, by maintaining the scarcity of artistic competence, those who possessed it could guarantee its cultural value.

For Bourdieu it now appeared that the French education system, as an instrument of those with the greatest capital accumulation (that equated to power), was organised to legitimise specific forms of culture as natural or superior (and by default making other forms of culture illegitimate and inferior) and to ensure that only those from families well endowed with capital would be effectively acculturated (Bourdieu and Johnson, 1993: 232). Furthermore, as in the earlier *Les héritiers* [Bourdieu and Passeron, 1964] (Bourdieu and Passeron, 1979), Bourdieu claimed that the education system tacitly discriminated against those who did not have the initial cultural competence to participate and led to those discriminated against automatically excluding themselves from education, thereby ensuring the reproduction of the cultural elite and the maintenance of the scarcity and value of cultural competence ('cultural' capital).

Towards the end of the essay Bourdieu re-presented the argument made in the conclusion of *L'amour de l'art* [Bourdieu, Darbel and Schnapper, 1966] (Bourdieu, Darbel and Schnapper, 1990): that educational reform offered a way to provide egalitarian access to legitimised culture:

> Only an institution like a school, the specific function of which is methodologically to develop or create the inclinations which produce an educated person and which lay the foundations, quantitatively and qualitatively, of a constant and intense pursuit of culture, could offset (at least partially) the initial disadvantage of those who do not receive from their family circle the encouragement to undertake cultural activities (**Bourdieu and Johnson, 1993: 233**).

However, only two years later Bourdieu came to the bleak conclusion, published in *La reproduction: Éléments pour une théorie du système d'enseignement* (*Reproduction in Education, Society and Culture*) [Bourdieu and Passeron, 1970] (Bourdieu and Passeron, 1977), that education was inevitably an instrument controlled by those in power and therefore would never operate in a manner that might threaten to erode that power. As a consequence Bourdieu subsequently revised his own political aims from contributing to the reform of education to helping the powerless to understand the 'hidden' mechanisms of their oppression.

Bourdieu came to the bleak conclusion ... that education was inevitably an instrument controlled by those in power and therefore would never operate in a manner that might threaten to erode that power.

Photography and aesthetic perception

During the mid-1960s Bourdieu undertook a large empirical study of the emerging practice of photography. Bourdieu was a keen photographer himself, as evidenced by his earlier publications on Algeria and he had already published the results of a small study of the photographic habits of the peasant community in his home province of Béarn [Bourdieu and Bourdieu, 1965] (Bourdieu and Bourdieu, 2004). As a result of his new association with the Centre for European Sociology Bourdieu was able to secure research funding from Kodak, who were keen to find out how the French were using their increasingly accessible products. For Bourdieu, a study of the relatively new yet ubiquitous practice of photography promised to provide insights into the aesthetic dispositions of the French population. The project itself consisted of a rather diverse set of studies carried out by a team of researchers that included: the use of photography within families; the ways that different social groups used photographs; a comparative analysis of camera clubs; and a study of professional photographers and their aesthetic dispositions. The results of these studies subsequently formed the main chapters in the second part of a book entitled *Un art moyen, essai sur les usages sociaux de la photographie (Photography: A Middle-brow Art)* [Bourdieu, Boltanski *et al.*, 1965] (Bourdieu, Boltanski *et al.*, 1989).

The results of this study further reinforced the central findings of Bourdieu's previous studies into aesthetic appreciation. Most importantly they confirmed a correlation between aesthetic dispositions, preferences and practices and social position, that is, photographic practices were a 'register' of social position. The empirical findings of the study appear very dated because they predated both the rise of high-art photography, which legitimised specific forms of photographic practice and dismissed others, and digitalisation, which increased the accessibility of photography. However, Bourdieu's contributions to the book, the Introduction (Bourdieu, Boltanski *et al.*, 1989: 1–10) and Part I (Bourdieu *et al.*, 1989: 13–72), provided a useful synopsis of both his emerging 'scientific' research method and his theory of the socio-political construction of aesthetics. It is particularly notable that the language of Bourdieu's text demonstrated a change from its previous emphasis on the way objective constraints, structures and rules, governed individual action, towards a new emphasis on the way that objective constraints and individual subjectivity worked together to produce cultural practices. This new understanding of the relationship between the objective and subjective was later reified in the seminal *Esquisse d'une théorie de la pratique* [1972a] (1977a).

… the language of Bourdieu's text demonstrated … a new emphasis on the way that objective constraints and individual subjectivity worked together to produce cultural practices.

In a chapter within Part I entitled 'The Social Definition of Photography' Bourdieu extrapolated the project's findings into a general theory of class-based aesthetics (Bourdieu *et al.*, 1989: 73–98). To a certain extent Bourdieu used his findings to reinforce his previous theoretical ideas about the correlation between aesthetics and capital – that is, those with more cultural, economic and social capital had the resources necessary to take part in the game of 'pure', 'disinterested' aesthetics, whereas those with few capital resources had no choice but to create a resource-bound aesthetics – which he subsequently termed the 'taste of necessity' (1984a: 374). Bourdieu also reiterated the notion, which first emerged in his Algerian research, that social groups constructed their own distinctive notions of aesthetics, thereby both reflecting and supporting the social cohesion of the group. However, in contradistinction to the tacit assumption contained in both *Les héritiers* and *L'amour de l'art* that 'pure' aesthetics were superior to 'popular' aesthetics, as evidenced by Bourdieu's repeated argument that the lower social group in society should be helped to appreciate 'high culture', Bourdieu now argued that, far from being 'vulgar', popular aesthetics had their own particular symbolic content and beauty:

> **The most banal tasks always include actions which owe nothing to the pure and simple quest for efficiency, and the actions most directly geared towards practical ends may elicit aesthetic judgements ... Thus, most of society can be excluded from the universe of legitimate culture without being excluded from the universe of aesthetics (Bourdieu, Boltanski *et al.*, 1989: 7–8).**

Further, Bourdieu proposed that 'popular' aesthetics should be appreciated as 'authentic', meaningful and of value to those groups who constructed them and should not be denigrated to the status of a structuralist 'foil' to high aesthetics or 'good taste'. Bourdieu's proposition was radical for the time and presaged the message that was later proffered by both post-modernist aesthetics and cultural studies (Garnham and Williams, 1980). Additionally, it appears that Bourdieu was suggesting that his earlier discovery of the symbolic sophistication of peasant societies might have equivalence in the working classes of western capitalist societies. Yet, while pointing to the genuine value of 'popular' aesthetics to the working classes, Bourdieu argued that 'popular' aesthetics were, in reality, constantly devalued by those in power (those with the most capital) via institutions that legitimised notions of 'pure', disinterested aesthetics (i.e. schools, museums, art galleries) (Bourdieu, Boltanski *et al.*, 1989: 95). However, whilst expounding the injustice of this situation, unlike in the reformist conclusions of *Les héritiers* and *L'amour de l'art*, Bourdieu now suggested that the sociologist's role should be 'concerned with deciphering that which is only ever *common sense*' (Bourdieu *et al.*, 1989: 9), thereby merely revealing the mechanisms that created social inequality in society.

... while pointing to the genuine value of the 'popular' aesthetics to the working classes Bourdieu argued that 'popular' aesthetics were, in reality, constantly devalued by those in power ...

Actes de la recherche en sciences sociales

By the close of the 1960s Bourdieu had established an empirical correlation between social position and aesthetic perception and practices in specific cases (art and photography). He had also developed a hypothesis suggesting that legitimised culture circulated as a form of capital in society and that cultural capital, like economic capital, was the object of social struggle and status. During the 1970s Bourdieu carried out further studies designed to broaden and deepen this hypothesis and in the mid-1970s he founded the journal *Actes de la recherche en sciences sociales*, which aimed to encourage and provide the 'voice-piece' for a wide-range of 'sociological' studies into everyday culture. Bourdieu contributed over eighty articles to the journal from 1975 to 2002. Throughout the 1970s Bourdieu also continued the development of his general theory of social practice and his sociological methodology through the reworking of his Algerian fieldwork, most notably in the counter-structuralist *Esquisse d'une théorie de la pratique* [1972a] (1977a) and its subsequent reconfiguration in *Le sens pratique* [1980c] (1990c). However, *Actes de la recherche en sciences sociales* acted as the main vehicle for the dissemination of the results of a series of theoretical and empirical studies exploring specifically cultural aspects of his theoretical ideas.

'The Market of Symbolic Goods'

In the essay 'Le marché des biens symboliques' ('The Market of Symbolic Goods') [1971c] (1985a) Bourdieu attempted to integrate his earlier notion of the social construction of art perception with his most recent conceptual tool:

'fields'. Bourdieu's notion of field, inspired by his reading of Weber's sociology of religion, first appeared in 'Champ intellectuel et projet créateur' [1966a] (1969) (1971a). Bourdieu suggested that the notion of field could be used to represent the 'autonomous', bounded, nature of a group of artists, buyers and intermediaries, who shared a constructed set of knowledge, beliefs and values, and who existed in a hierarchical, capital dependent, juxtaposition with other social groups (fields) in social space. 'Le marché des biens symboliques' extended Bourdieu's previous characterisation by suggesting that cultural fields were divided into two 'fractions'. First, there was the small 'field of restricted production' (FRP), an autonomous field in which well-educated consumers shared the codes of aesthetic appreciation with well-educated producers. Second, there was the much larger 'field of large-scale production' (FLP), a field in which less well educated producers responded to the demands of the 'popular', and largely uneducated market. Bourdieu also argued that, given the causal relationship between scarcity and value, both consumers and producers within both fractions of the field adopted strategies which would, they calculated, lead to 'distinction'; i.e. an increase in their cultural capital and their standing in the field.

[Bourdieu suggested] that cultural fields were divided into two 'fractions'… the 'field of restricted production' … and the 'field of large-scale production' …

'The Anatomy of Taste'

Bourdieu's status within the field of international sociology increased during the 1970s, which meant that he was able to obtain the funding for a large and ambitious study into the cultural tastes and practices of the French public. The results of this study were first published in an article, 'Anatomie du goût' ('Anatomy of Taste'), in *Actes de la recherche en sciences sociales* in 1976 [Bourdieu and Saint-Martin, 1976: 2–81], which some two years later formed the core of the Bourdieu's best-known book, *La distinction: critique sociale du jugement* (*Distinction: A Social Critique of the Judgement of Taste*) [1979b] (1984a). In 'Anatomie du goût' Bourdieu presented the findings from over 1,000 questionnaires and interviews carried out during 1963 and between 1967 and 1968, and from official government statistical data. The results of the study provided a stark *exposé* of French cultural tastes and practices and the ways that cultural institutions, particularly schools, reinforced cultural and social divisions in French society. The findings confirmed the results of Bourdieu's previous small studies and allowed him to test and develop his tentative theory of practice (the interrelation between *habitus*, field and capital) in relation to the cultural field. The English synopsis to the online article pronounced that the study aimed:

> **to construct and verify a systematic theory of the *habitus*, conceived both as a system of schemes producing homologous effects in very different domains and as a way of mediating between the space of social positions and the space of life styles [Bourdieu and Saint-Martin, 1976: 2].**

That is, he wanted to explore whether his understanding of class-based aesthetic dispositions (or tastes), which he had previously developed in relation to the perception and consumption of art, could be extended to account for all cultural goods and practices (or lifestyles). The answer to this question was a most emphatic and resounding 'yes', and the article presented detailed statistical and ethnographic data on a vast range of cultural issues to prove his point. For instance, the study asked respondents to express the characteristics of their 'ideal home' from a predetermined list, consisting of adjectives ranging from 'clean and tidy' at one extreme through 'cosy' and 'comfortable' to 'harmonious' and 'studied' at the other extreme.

[Bourdieu] wanted to explore whether his understanding of class-based aesthetic dispositions (or tastes) ... could be extended to account for all cultural goods and practices (or lifestyles).

The results were correlated against the respondents' job type and, perhaps not surprisingly, they demonstrated that the working-class respondents expressed preferences for functional interiors, the middle classes wanted 'cosy', 'comfortable' and 'neat' interiors, while the most-educated classes, teachers and professionals, preferred more aesthetic, 'studied' and 'harmonious' homes [Bourdieu and Saint-Martin, 1976: 33] (Bourdieu, 1984a: 248). These rather dry statistics were complimented by a series of fascinating biographical vignettes describing the lifestyles and interior preferences of a number of respondents [Bourdieu and Saint-Martin, 1976: 38] (Bourdieu, 1984a: 268, 274, 298, 321, 324, 334, 391). The following example is typical: 'He likes "modern things" and would have liked "white furniture" but doesn't like the English style his wife favours (she would like to own "a big dresser with a collection of plates")' (Bourdieu, 1984a: 334).

One of the most innovative parts of Bourdieu's article was the synthetic 'mapping' of the relative positions of respondents in social space by vocation, as defined by their total capital and the configuration of their economic and cultural capital (Bourdieu and Saint-Martin, 1976: 10–11) (Bourdieu, 1984a: 128–9) (see Figure 7). In this diagram social space was defined by two axes: the horizontal axis represented the configuration (relative volumes) of economic and cultural capital, while the vertical axis represented the total volume of capital (economic plus cultural capital). Aware that his map might be misread as suggesting that social positions were static, when in fact they changed over time, Bourdieu added an arrow against each vocation, representing the social trajectory over time. Thus, as an example, 'Artistic producers' and 'higher education teachers' appeared in the top-left quadrant because they had relatively little economic capital but significant cultural capital and so their total capital volume was relatively high; and further, the forty-five-degree upwardly pointing arrow suggested that they were likely to improve their social positions over time. Bourdieu had effectively produced a three-dimensional relational map of society. However, he did not stop there. The map that appeared in *Actes de la recherche en sciences sociales* [Bourdieu and Saint-Martin, 1976: 10–11] included a tracing-paper overlay, 'The Space of Lifestyles' (reproduced on page 47), containing the study's research data on the lifestyle practices of the

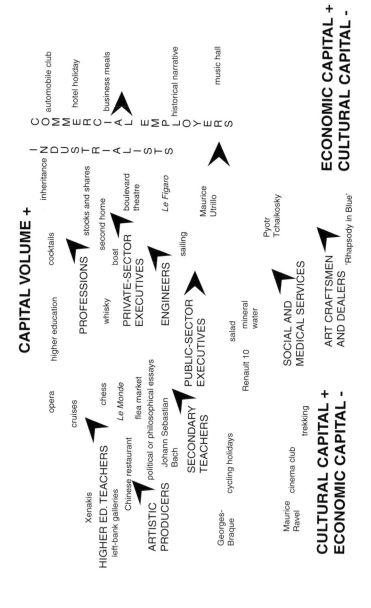

CAPITAL VOLUME +

CULTURAL CAPITAL +
ECONOMIC CAPITAL -

ECONOMIC CAPITAL +
CULTURAL CAPITAL -

INDUSTRIALISTS

COMMERCIAL EMPLOYERS

automobile club
hotel holiday
business meals
historical narrative
music hall
inheritance
stocks and shares
second home
boulevard theatre
Le Figaro
Maurice Utrillo
Pyotr Tchaikosky
sailing
cocktails
whisky
boat
opera
higher education
mineral water
salad
Renault 10
chess
Le Monde
flea market
political or philosophical essays
Johann Sebastian Bach
Xenakis
left-bank galleries
Chinese restaurant
cycling holidays
Maurice Ravel
cinema club
trekking
'Rhapsody in Blue'

PROFESSIONS
PRIVATE-SECTOR EXECUTIVES
ENGINEERS
PUBLIC-SECTOR EXECUTIVES
SECONDARY TEACHERS
HIGHER ED. TEACHERS
ARTISTIC PRODUCERS
SOCIAL AND MEDICAL SERVICES
ART CRAFTSMEN AND DEALERS
Georges-Braque

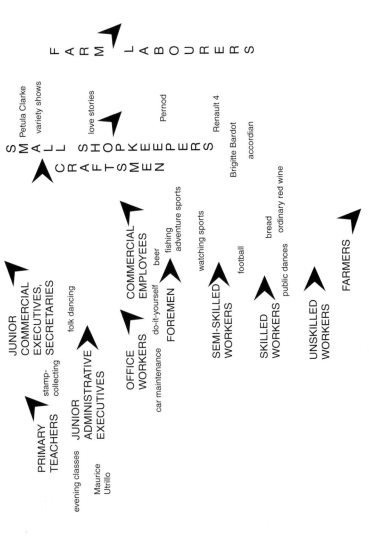

Figure 7 The space of social positions/the space of lifestyles, after the diagram of the same name in *Distinction* (Bourdieu, 1984a: 128–9).

respondents distributed along the same two axes (in *La distinction* the two maps were superimposed) (Bourdieu, 1984a: 128–9). The overlaying of the 'The Space of Lifestyles' on to 'The Space of Social Positions' demonstrated remarkable correlations between vocations, capital and lifestyle choices. The combined diagram suggested, for instance, that artistic producers frequented left-bank galleries, enjoyed Chinese food and read political or philosophical essays, whereas foremen liked fishing, beer, car-maintenance and watching sports. John Frow subsequently questioned some of the assumptions that underpinned the diagram, for example, the possibility of adding economic (material) capital and cultural (metaphorical) capital together to form 'total capital'; that 'social capital' was deemed irrelevant (although this might have been the case in France); and that volumes of cultural capital could be correlated directly with levels of education (1995: 39–40) (1987: 67). Despite these valid reservations, Bourdieu's diagram demonstrated that his conceptual framework was moving away from his previous and very crude class-based taxonomy of society to a much more convincing relational model. Yet, rather disappointingly, in the text that followed the diagram, Bourdieu reverted to his class-based taxonomy and discussed the study's research findings in relation to three classes of taste, bourgeois taste, petit bourgeois taste and working-class taste, and their interrelations. For instance, Bourdieu characterised the petite bourgeoisie as the 'aspiring' class who attempted to imitate the tastes of the bourgeoisie, through, for instance, the purchase of reproduction furniture, but who lacked the resources or levels of acculturation to join them. Bourdieu's text also hung on to the binary notion, derived from structuralism, that the characteristics of bourgeois taste were defined in opposition to working-class taste (high–low, pure–vulgar, disinterested–functional). Although this notion clearly had some evidential base, it failed to acknowledge that the working classes could and did construct their own aesthetic values that might or might not have been constructed in relation to bourgeois taste. Several commentators have subsequently remarked that Bourdieu, despite being on the side of the oppressed, curiously spent very little time trying to understand working-class culture on its own terms (Frow, 1987) (Frow, 1995) (Fiske, 1991) (Honneth, 1986).

Bourdieu characterised the petite bourgeoisie as the 'aspiring'

class who attempted to imitate the tastes of the bourgeoisie

… but lacked the resources or acculturation to join them.

Bourdieu's preference for understanding bourgeois and petit bourgeois taste was reflected in a second ambitious diagram. This time Bourdieu attempted to produce a graphic representation portraying the relationship between dominant (bourgeois) and petit bourgeois tastes, inherited capital and vocational fields [Bourdieu and Saint-Martin, 1976: 46, 68] (Bourdieu, 1984a: 262, 340) (see Figure 8). The diagram employed two axes: the horizontal axis represented the configuration of economic and cultural capital held by individuals and the vertical axis represented their relative seniority within the bourgeoisie (using their father's profession as an indicator of seniority). Respondents were located on the diagram in a position that related to their seniority and the configuration of their cultural and economic capitals. Then, as with the previous diagram (Figure 7), Bourdieu superimposed the tastes and aesthetic preferences of the respondents to produce a map of 'Variants of the dominant taste (Bourdieu, 1984a: 262, 340). Further, the diagram that appeared in *Actes de la recherche en sciences sociales* [Bourdieu and Saint-Martin, 1976: 46, 68] included an additional tracing-paper overlay that indicated the spatial boundaries for respondents from a number of different vocational fields. Unfortunately, the diagram that appeared in *La distinction* superimposed the two layers making the diagram difficult to read (Bourdieu, 1984a: 262) (Figure 8). Nevertheless, the resulting diagram provided a fascinating graphic representation of the socio-spatial boundaries of vocation-related fields, the aesthetic tastes and practices of those located within fields, and the relational positions of fields in social space. Importantly, Bourdieu's accompanying text reminded the reader that the diagram represented a sociologist's model of reality, which should not be mistaken for reality itself.

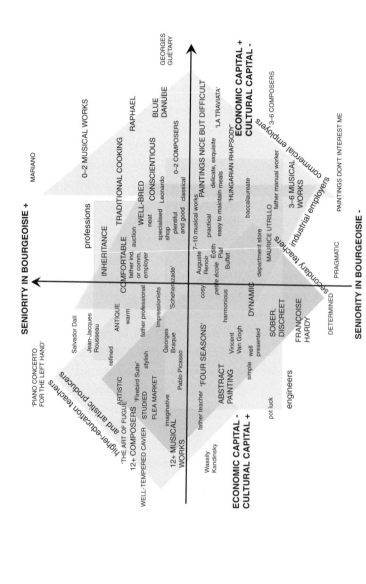

Figure 8 Variants of the dominant taste: the space of properties and the space of individuals, after the diagram of the same name in *Distinction* (Bourdieu, 1984a: 262).

Bourdieu's opus *La distinction: critique sociale du jugement* (*Distinction: A Social Critique of the Judgement of Taste*) was first published in 1979 [1979b] [1984a]. The book immediately became a bestseller among the French liberal middle classes who found the message particularly resonant. Bourdieu stated that the aim of the book was to provide

> **a scientific answer to the old question of Kant's critique of judgement, by**
> **seeking in the structure of the social classes the basis of the systems of**
> **classification which structure perception of the social world and designate the**
> **objects of aesthetic enjoyment (Bourdieu, 1984a: xii–xiv).**

In addition to providing evidence to support the hypothesis that aesthetic codes were socially constructed, Bourdieu also asserted that he wanted to prove that 'art and cultural consumption are predisposed, consciously and deliberately or not, to fulfil a social function of legitimating social differences' (1984a: 7).

In effect Bourdieu wanted to challenge those who were complicit in, and benefited from, Kantian aesthetics, namely the intellectual classes, by revealing what was really going on. For readers conversant with Bourdieu's previous work *La distinction* was disappointing because it consisted of a melange of reworked papers from the 1960s and 1970s, which appeared to lack any overarching intellectual coherence or clarity. Yet, the huge book, consisting of over 600 pages of photographs, interview transcripts, illustrative maps and diagrams, succeeded, if only because it allowed Bourdieu to disseminate to a broad public audience his challenging propositions on the social construction of taste and, more importantly, the role of taste in the maintenance of social inequality in French society.

Bourdieu wanted to challenge those who were complicit in, and benefited from, Kantian aesthetics, namely the intellectual classes, by revealing what was really going on.

Many of the chapters that were brought together to form *La distinction* have been discussed in the correct chronological order, demonstrating the development of Bourdieu's ideas on aesthetics, in the previous pages of this chapter. However, given that the reader might find it easier to access *La distinction* than the original papers it might be useful to know that: Part I reworked 'Le marché des biens symboliques' [1971c] and 'Éléments d'une théorie sociologique de la perception artistique' from 1968 [1968b]; Parts II and III contained an edited version of 'Anatomie du goût' [Bourdieu and Saint-Martin, 1976], but including more illustrative material than the original article; Chapter 8 republished 'Les doxosophes' ('Thoughtless Thought') from 1972 [1972b]; while Appendix IV republished 'Un jeu chinois' ('A Parlour Game') from 1976 [1976]. In fact, the only wholly new text in *La distinction* was the postscript at the end of the book entitled 'Towards a "Vulgar" Critique of "Pure" Critiques' (1984a: 485–500). Bourdieu began the postscript by restating his belief that the Kantian notions of 'pure' aesthetics, and its foil 'vulgar' aesthetics, were nothing more than the illusory constructions of a cultural elite, which had the effect of reifying the distinction between the dominant and dominated groups in society. Bourdieu followed this accusation with an attack on intellectuals for their self-serving complicity with this situation. He proceeded by using Jacques Derrida's famous critique of Kant, *La vérité en peinture*, as a paradigmatic example of the way intellectuals, however radical they claimed to be, actually perpetuated the constructs of their intellectual field because they feared the loss of their own position in the internal struggle for power. Intellectuals, Bourdieu claimed, had a powerful vested interest in perpetuating the social game that would lead to their own rise to distinction. Bourdieu went on to expand this argument in relation to the field of literature and art in *Les règles de l'art* [1992] (see Chapter 4).

Bourdieu insisted throughout his career that he was not a theoretician, but rather, that his empirical studies tested hypothetical constructs, which attempted to account for reality. Thereby the results of his studies served to continuously expand, test and revise his constructs. In effect Bourdieu's whole oeuvre was orientated towards the production of a universal account of social practice and his work on French taste was merely part of this larger project. Bourdieu argued at the end of the preface to the English-language edition of *Distinction* that it was necessary for other studies to be carried out by other researchers, in other cultures and at other times, as a means of both testing and extending his 'tentative' theory of social practice (1984a: xiv). In a lecture to a Japanese audience in 1991 he asserted his belief that the invariant logic of social practice could only revealed through studying the context specific manifestations of practice: 'the deepest logic of the social world can be grasped only if one plunges into the plurality of empirical reality, historically located and dated but with the objective of constructing it as a special case of what is possible' (1991b: 628).

Rather disappointingly, few sociologists took up his challenge and the only subsequent substantial studies on the social construction of taste were a study of Australian taste by Tony Bennett, Michael Emmison and John Frow (1999) and a study of British taste by Tony Bennett *et al.* (2009).

Bourdieu argued ... that it was necessary for other studies to be carried out by other researchers, in other cultures and at other times, as a means of both testing and extending his 'tentative' theory of social practice.

These studies broadly adopted Bourdieu research methodology although in the analysis of their data they paid more attention to the intersections of class with gender, age and race, reflecting the sociological concerns of their time.

Following the publication of *La distinction*, Bourdieu largely turned his attention to investigating the socio-historical production of culture in both historical and contemporary contexts. These investigations included a study of the socio-genesis of literary and artistic field in nineteenth-century Paris, which resulted in the publication of *Les règles de l'art* [1992] (1996a), and empirical studies on a number of contemporary fields of cultural production including fashion, sport, politics and academia. Bourdieu also became involved in a series of high-profile public protests against the inequalities of neo-liberal capitalism. These included a series of articles and books on journalism, the mass media and particularly on television [1996b] (1998d). In these writings Bourdieu identified the loosening grip by the French state on culture and the increasing influence of commercialisation and the mass media (digital, cable, satellite). Bourdieu's analysis of the effect of these changes on society was very critical. He argued that, far from facilitating a diversity of cultural production which might cater for the cultural tastes of a broad range of cultural groups in society, the mass media had shamelessly distorted and exploited the market for the sake of maximising profit. For, instance he chastised reality television as a cynical media ploy to maximise the number of viewers and minimise the cost of production by merely feeding reality back to the viewer [1996b] (1998d). However, Bourdieu's tacit preference for high culture over popular culture, together with the lack of empirical evidence to support his claims, made his arguments appear overly subjective. Several commentators have subsequently suggested that Bourdieu's greatest weaknesses were the paucity of his attempts to understand the diversity or sophistication of popular culture, and his failure to recognise the capacity for resistance that existed in certain sub-fields of popular culture (such as music and graffiti) (Frow, 1985) (Frow, 1997) (Fiske, 1991) (Honneth, 1986) (Prior, 2005).

Buying houses – 'the taste of fantasy'

One of Bourdieu's last large sociological studies, published initially in a themed edition of *Actes de la recherche en sciences sociales* [Bourdieu, Christin *et al.*, 1990] and subsequently in book form as *Les structures sociales de l'économie* (*The Social Structures of the Economy*) [2000a] (2005a), employed his theory of practice as a means to understand the dynamics of the French housing market in Val d'Oise. The study involved collecting statistical data, including interviews with developers and house buyers, with the aim of demonstrating how and why the French housing market was shifting from rented, high-density housing to owner-occupied single-family houses during the early 1980s.

Bourdieu identified the new role that credit and advertising played in tempting the working classes to move beyond the 'taste of necessity' and to indulge in the 'taste of fantasy'.

Bourdieu's analysis suggested that this shift was a result of the confluence of a number of contingencies: government housing policy, the new availability of credit, the competition between mass house-builders, and the use of class-orientated advertising tactics (2005a: 54–63). The chapters of the book analysed different aspects of this phenomenon. The chapter that looked at the taste of buyers, 'The Agent and the Field of Production' (2005a: 19–39), reported that people used a combination of social (cohesion of the family), cultural (symbolic) and economic (monetary value) criteria to select housing, and that the criteria differed in weight and manifestation for different social groups, thus confirming his previous findings on the social construction of taste. In a significant development from his previous findings Bourdieu identified the new role that credit and advertising played in tempting the working classes to move beyond the 'taste of necessity' (1984a: 374) and to indulge in the 'taste of fantasy', in this case the fantasy of semi-detached suburban living. The study went on to demonstrate that the consequences of home ownership for working-class buyers were often negative as, very quickly after the purchase, they came to realise that their seduction had resulted in, amongst other things, an unmanageable burden of debt (2005a: 185–92) (see Chapter 5 for a further discussion). This study deserves to be better known because its findings pointed to the radically new effect that access to credit was having on working-class and middle-class taste and consumption in the 1980s.

Postface

Although readers might find the empirical data presented in Bourdieu's publications on taste rather dated, arguably his conceptual tools (*habitus*, field and capital) and scientific, 'reflexive', methodology have proved to have continuing purchase as means of explaining and exploring the complexity of contemporary cultural tastes and practices (Prior, 2005) (Bennett, Emmison and Frow, 1999) (Bennett *et al.*, 2009). However, while Bourdieu's project has been extended by numerous studies carried out within the field of cultural studies, to date, with the exception of articles by Kim Dovey (Hillier and Rookesby, 2005: 283–96), Dennis Mann (1980) and Hélène Lipstadt (2001), there has been little interest shown in the field of architecture. Yet Bourdieu's work on taste challenges architects in many ways. Most importantly, it asks architects to consider how they might reconcile the potential schisms between their own taste culture and the taste cultures of those who inhabit architecture.

CHAPTER 4

Towards a Theory of Cultural Practice

Bourdieu's work on cultural production was never as well known as his work on cultural consumption. Yet, for Bourdieu, cultural production, consumption and reproduction were processes that were inextricably intertwined in the world of lived experiences. Consequentially, any plausible theory of practice had to account for the existence and interdependence of all three. That is, a theoretical model of action had to account for the relationship between practices and the contexts within which those practices occurred. Bourdieu's studies of culture, which included science, law and religion, as well as expressive aesthetic activities such as art, literature and music, were central to the development of his general theory of practice. Over the fifty or so years of his research he carried out a sustained programme of both empirical and socio-historical studies on cultural production. This work focused largely on a number of sub-fields including literature, art, photography, housing and fashion. Additionally, towards the end of his life he published a number of polemical critiques of television and journalism [1996b] (1998d: 70–7) (Bourdieu, 2008: 321–3, 333–9).

This chapter discusses the genesis of Bourdieu's theory of cultural production and the associated conceptual tools. The subsequent chapter introduces the reader to a number of Bourdieu's empirical case studies which tested, expanded and revised his theoretical model of cultural production. Together this work demonstrated Bourdieu's ongoing struggle to understand the relationship between individual action and social context and thereby to both resolve the theoretical tension between objectivism and subjectivism, and to expose the 'hidden' symbolic mechanisms in society that informed cultural production and supported social inequalities.

In 1964 Bourdieu moved from his teaching position in Lille to take up positions as lecturer at the École normale supérieure and Director of Studies at the École pratique des hautes études en sciences sociales, and to join the research group led by Jean-Claude Passeron and Raymond Aron at the Centre for European Sociology in Paris. The newly formed centre was a key part of Raymond Aron's mission to consolidate the emerging academic disciple of sociology.

Bourdieu, in conjunction with Jean-Claude Passeron and Jean-Claude Chamboredon, published *Le métier de sociologue* ... in 1968, that subsequently became a core textbook for sociological research in France.

Central to the centre's activities were two intertwined programmes of research. First, there was the programme to devise a robust 'sociological method' that would underpin research carried out within the new academic discipline. To that end Bourdieu, in conjunction with Jean-Claude Passeron and Jean-Claude Chamboredon, published *Le métier de sociologue: Préalables épistémologiques* (*The Craft of Sociology: Epistemological Preliminaries*) in 1968, that subsequently became a core textbook on research methods for sociology in France [Bourdieu, Chamboredon and Passeron, 1968] (Bourdieu, Chamboredon and Passeron, 1991). Second, there was the ambitious research agenda to explore explicitly sociological themes including the phenomenon of social mobility and the emergence of mass culture. Fortuitously, many of the resulting projects gained financial support from the government because they promised to provide data that would inform the government's reconstruction and modernisation policies (in which education and culture played key roles). This research environment provided Bourdieu with the opportunity to test the extent to which his understanding of the role of culture in society, based largely on his studies of homogeneous, pre-capitalist Kabyle society, might have efficacy in the heterogeneous society of capitalist France.

Photographic practice

During the 1960s Bourdieu carried out a number of sociological studies on cultural production, consumption and reproduction. While, as discussed in the previous chapter, his earlier work on students [Bourdieu and Passeron, 1964] (Bourdieu and Passeron, 1979) and museum attendance [Bourdieu, Darbel and Schnapper, 1966a] (Bourdieu, Darbel and Schnapper, 1990) had focused primarily on cultural consumption, Bourdieu's new study of photography focused on exploring photographic practice as a cultural practice.

In the early 1960s Bourdieu had carried out a small study on the social use of photography by peasants in his home province of Béarn (Bourdieu and Bourdieu, 1965). The revealing results of this research prompted Bourdieu to undertake a much larger collaborative study of contemporary French photographic practice, the results of which were published in *Un art moyen, essai sur les usages sociaux de la photographie* (*Photography: A Middle-brow Art*) [Bourdieu, Boltanski, Castel *et al.*, 1965] (Bourdieu, Boltanski, Castel *et al.*, 1989). This research, which collected data from interviews and questionnaires carried out in 1963 with 692 subjects living in Paris, Lille and a small French provincial town, and from other official sources (1989: 176 n.7), looked at the relationship between social status and photographic practices and the emerging practices of camera clubs and professional photographers. Bourdieu was interested in photography because it was, at that time, an emerging unconsecrated art form and therefore photographs were not yet 'valued' on the basis of 'official', 'established' or 'legitimised' criteria. Therefore, the study provided Bourdieu with a vehicle for revealing authentic, class-based, aesthetic values.

In Part I of *Un art moyen* Bourdieu outlined his theory of aesthetic perception, while Part II reported on the findings of interviews with three 'deviant' groups of photographers, professional photographers, photographic artists and photographic club members, whose practices Bourdieu suggested surpassed the naïve (Bourdieu, Boltanski, Castel *et al.*, 1989: 104). The first chapter in Part II, 'Aesthetic Ambitions and Social Ambitions: The Camera Club as a Secondary Group' (written by Robert Castel and Dominique Schnapper) described how camera clubs adopted various norms, values and rules, which were more explicit and circumscribed than naïve practices, as a means of securing and maintaining group cohesion.

Bourdieu was interested in photography because it was, at that time, an emerging unconsecrated art form and therefore photographs were not yet 'valued' by any 'official', 'established' or 'legitimised' criteria.

Bourdieu had, in the Introduction to the book, characterised these norms, values and rules collectively as a guiding '*ethos*' in the following way:

> via the medium of the *ethos* ... the group places this practice under its collective rule so that the most trivial photograph expresses, apart from the explicit intentions of the photographer, the system of schemes of perception, thought and appreciation common to the whole group (Bourdieu, Boltanski, Castel *et al.*, 1989: 6).

Castel and Schnapper also found a strong correlation between the content and emphasis of a club's *ethos* and the social class of its membership. For instance, clubs with working-class members tended to give pre-eminence to technical sophistications whereas those with highly educated members tended to give pre-eminence to aesthetic novelty. The authors attributed the flourishing of such diversity to the newness of the art and the consequential lack of consecrated norms, values and beliefs which would otherwise provide a measure of what constituted legitimate photographic practice.

The second chapter in Part II, 'Mechanical Art, Natural Art: Photographic Artists', was written by Jean-Claude Chamboredon and reported on the practices of artists who used photography in their work. Chamboredon's study found that artists transferred their prior learned artistic *ethos* to their photographic practice.

The final chapter in Part II, 'Professional Men or Men of Quality: Professional Photographers', written by Chamboredon and Bourdieu, reported on the results of a survey of 200 professional photographers. The survey found that there were factors that unified the emerging professionals, but there were also significant differences. The common perceptions included: a fear of competition from amateur photographers; a lack of group cohesion – they were found to be individualistic, isolated, jealous, independent (Bourdieu, Boltanski, Castel *et al.*, 1989: 148–9); and a shared desire to establish a recognised profession with the associated professional status and rewards. However, the study also found a great diversity in aesthetic practice and that the form of practice correlated closely with levels of educational achievement. The study concluded that individual educational achievement was the most significant factor in determining individual practice.

Together, the studies of the three 'deviant' groups revealed a diverse range of aesthetic practices that appeared to reflect the various social positions of the practitioners/clubs in the broader social space/field. Bourdieu ascribed this diversity to the newness of the profession and the consequential absence of recognised training, qualifications, gateways to practice, or legitimised notions of aesthetic practice. As a result Bourdieu suggested that, while there was a homology between the social origin of professional photographic practitioners and their markets, there was no established notion of 'high' photographic practice, or its corollary, 'popular' photographic practice, because no group had yet claimed legitimacy for one form over another. Clearly, as Grenfell subsequently noted, the world of photographic practice changed dramatically in the latter half of the twentieth century. These changes were: the advent of photography courses; new forms of digital technology; the rise of media versus art practices; and the ubiquity of the form, which collectively led to the field's reconfiguration and increasing alignment with other longer established fields of cultural production (Grenfell and Hardy, 2007: 169–70).

Bourdieu suggested that ... there was no established notion of 'high' photographic practice, or its corollary, 'popular' photographic practice, because no group had yet claimed legitimacy for one form over another.

Bourdieu's study of photographic practice might best be understood, first, as a vehicle for the development of his general theory of practice, and second, as presenting a snapshot of a historical moment. This study reinforced Bourdieu's hypothesis that people in society formed groups sharing the same world view and the same 'arbitrary' *ethos* (a term more procedural than the earlier 'ethic' but less dispositional than it the later *habitus*) reflecting their pre-existing position in social space.

Parallel socio-historical studies

During the 1960s Bourdieu consulted literature from the history of art to inform his sociological studies of the cultural preferences of museum attendees and university students, and the practice of photography. This literature also informed four historical papers [1966a] [1966b] [1967] (1968a) that together represented the embryonic origins of Bourdieu's theory of cultural practice. Derek Robbins has suggested that these were the first of Bourdieu's papers not to be explicitly linked with the findings of empirical research and that they 'were an indication that Bourdieu was theoretically taking stock of his position' (1991: 61). As an example, 'Outline of a Sociological Theory of Art Perception' (1968a) proposed an explicitly anti-Kantian theory of art appreciation which, in presenting a politicised reading of Erwin Panofsky's work on iconography and meaning (Panofsky, 1939; 1955), contended that the ability to produce and decode art was learned, or socially constructed, rather than being an innate or 'natural' ability. He also suggested that art appreciation and production were part of the same mutually reinforcing mechanism that contributed to the maintenance of hierarchies in society. The most ambitious and wide-ranging of the four papers was 'Champ intellectuel et projet créateur' ('The Intellectual Field and the Creative Project'), which first reached an English-speaking readership in 1969 [1966a] (1969) (1971a).

Genesis of the field of cultural production

Bourdieu began 'Champ intellectuel et projet créateur' with the claim that artists and intellectuals acted within semi-autonomous social spaces, which he termed cultural fields, where practice was guided by commonly held beliefs and values.

However, Bourdieu rejected any essential, trans-historical or trans-national notion of cultural fields and clearly stated that, although fields might share invariant structural characteristics, their objective configurations at any point in time and space were socio-historically contingent.

Bourdieu began ... with the claim that artists and intellectuals acted within semi-autonomous social spaces ... where practice was guided by commonly held beliefs and values.

Bourdieu proceeded to set out his own account of the historical genesis of the autonomous French artistic field. He argued that throughout the Middle Ages, the Renaissance and the Classical periods, artists were controlled by an external legitimising authority (variously the church, the aristocracy and the state) who dictated art production including its subject matter, form and style. Bourdieu then claimed, drawing heavily on L. L. Schücking's account of the genesis of the autonomous field of French literature (1998), that, during the nineteenth century, artists took steps to liberate themselves from external control. He suggested that artists gradually achieved semi-autonomy by constructing a field with an internal market for its products by tapping into the capital and thirst for novelty demonstrated by the burgeoning bourgeoisie and its associated critics, art dealers, salons and art galleries. Bourdieu characterised this field as consisting of agents who shared the same world view but were nevertheless engaged in internal struggles for legitimacy and control over what could be said and done within the field. He wrote: 'the intellectual field becomes an increasingly complex system, increasingly independent of external influences ... a field of relations governed by a specific logic: competition for cultural legitimacy' (1969: 71).

Alongside the development of an autonomous artistic field Bourdieu identified the rise of a new kind of artist, one who did not 'wish to recognize any obligations other than the intrinsic demands of his own creative project' (1969: 91), that is, one who produced 'art for art's sake', or 'pure' aesthetics. Further, Bourdieu suggested that the moral and ethical superiority that was associated with this new artistic quest resulted in the notion of 'pure' aesthetics becoming the pre-eminent value in the 'arbitrary' field-specific configuration of values (or capitals; economic, cultural and social). As a result the internal struggles within the artistic field would revolve around who could claim authority over aesthetic matters. Bourdieu concluded the section by re-stating that the role of the researcher was to uncover 'the historical and social conditions which make possible the existence of an intellectual field' in any historical moment and to understand the 'concrete totality of the relations that constitute the intellectual field as a system' (1969: 95). Bourdieu subsequently expanded his socio-genesis of the field of artistic production, particularly in relation to the literary field, in a series of essays written in the 1980s, culminating in a synoptic book, *Les règles de l'art*, that was published in 1992 [1992] (1996a) (see Chapter 5).

Artists and their audience

In the second part of 'Champ intellectuel et projet créateur' [1966a], 'The Birds of Psaphon' (1969: 95–105), Bourdieu identified the relationship of mutual dependency between artists and their audiences within the field of artistic production.

Bourdieu suggested that an artist's work was inevitably the product of a dialectic between 'the intrinsic necessity of the work of art' … and the 'social pressures which directed the work from the outside'.

He suggested that artists, writers and intellectuals produced work for a perceived audience but that they only had a weak control over the actual audience response to their work; that is, whether their work would be well received or not. In addition, Bourdieu identified the potential for a misalignment between the artist's self-perception and that held by society when he wrote:

> The artist may accept or reject the image of himself which society reflects back at him, he cannot ignore it ... society intervenes at the very centre of the creative project thrusting upon the artist its demands and refusals, its expectations and its indifference (1969: 95).

Bourdieu went on to suggest that an artist's work was inevitably the product of a dialectic between 'the intrinsic necessity of the work of art' (1969: 163), the artist's own intention for the work, and the 'social pressures which directed the work from outside' (1969: 96), that is, the artist's perceptions of the aesthetic preferences of the audience.

He also suggested that, in practice, the resolution of this dialectic ranged from, at one extreme, work being produced to satisfy perceived audience expectations (one thinks, for example, of bestselling authors who become trapped by the necessity to serve the tastes of their established readership) and at the other extreme avant-garde work being produced with the aim of creating new audiences. Yet, Bourdieu pointed out that in all cases artists worked within the historically derived contemporary logic of their own field and that art was always conceived and received in relation to the projects of other artists, both past and present: 'the most singular and personal aesthetic judgement has reference to a common meaning already established' (1969: 104).

Bourdieu went on to suggest that the aim of all artists was to produce work that, by means of its recognised value, would increase their cultural capital and thereby improve their position in the field. He also pointed to the ways that 'cultural intermediaries' such as critics, publishers and gallery owners, had the power to be 'taste makers' by mediating between artists and audiences within the field (1969: 100). Bourdieu explained how the interpretations and judgements made by cultural intermediaries could work in a partisan way to support the upward trajectory of certain artists or to dismiss others (1971a: 170). The successful artist was therefore one who optimally combined what he/she wanted to say with a sufficient element of what he/she anticipated that critics would be predisposed to esteem.

Field mechanisms

In the third part of 'Champ intellectuel et projet créateur', 'Prophets, Priests and Sorcerers' (1969: 105–12), Bourdieu attempted to define the structure, later to be renamed 'logic', of the field of artistic production. Building on the previous section Bourdieu characterised the field as a social space in which various interdependent agents, artists, critics, etc., competed for the authority to define what was considered of artistic value, legitimacy or orthodoxy. But, despite maintaining that competitive struggles were characteristic in all fields Bourdieu, after Weber, insisted that there was a concomitant functional complicity within fields, that is, an underlying shared belief in the existence of the field and its aims, which ensured its continuing existence.

Bourdieu characterised the field as a social space in which various interdependent agents ... competed for the authority to define what was considered of artistic value, legitimacy or orthodoxy.

Bourdieu went on to maintain that all artists worked within context-specific cultural field configurations that gave precedence to some forms of culture over others (for instance, in the 1960s opera and poetry were recognised as legitimate forms of culture but photography was struggling to gain legitimacy). Yet, artists existed in relation to each other in the social space of the field and their relative positions reflected the quantity and configuration of their capital (social, economic and cultural). Those with the most cultural capital, which was recognised internally as the pre-eminent capital in the field, had the power to define what constituted legitimate culture (form and content) and those with less cultural capital fought to gain legitimacy for their beliefs and thereby overturn those in power. Bourdieu then described the way that a newcomer would enter the field of cultural production for the first time and the way that their pre-existing capital (social, cultural and economic) configuration would place them in a field position that reflected the value that the new field placed on each form of capital. The newcomer would subsequently adopt a course of action that they perceived would improve their position in the field and move them towards appropriating the power to control the field. Bourdieu's notion of the economy of practices provided a fundamental challenge to the altruistic notions that pervaded artistic practice at the time and, to an alarming extent, continue to exist today.

Bourdieu's text also proposed a relational model that could account for the interrelation between the artistic field and other fields. He suggested that the artistic field mediated social relations between itself and other fields in the social world by refracting external field structures according to its own internal structure. By extension it followed that the relationship which artists had with 'social reality outside the intellectual field was [also] mediated by the structure of the intellectual field' (1971a: 177). This insightful notion accounted for the way members from different fields (or social groups) perceived objects in multiple and often contrary ways.

Bourdieu ended the section by suggesting that a monopoly over the legitimation of contemporary art and artists was exercised by the Academy. He also pointed out the paradoxical situation whereby contemporary artists sought consecration from the very institution whose orthodoxy they sought to overturn. Finally, and reiterating Bourdieu's earlier discussion of Derrida's work (1984a: 486–500), he pointed out that, while artists often claimed to be fighting fundamental ideological battles that challenged the very existence of the artistic field, they were merely fighting to better their own position, because, in reality, no artist would set out to undermine the source of their own status and power.

[Bourdieu] pointed out that, while artists often claimed to be fighting fundamental ideological battles that challenged the very existence of the artistic field, they were merely fighting to better their own position.

The conscious and the unconscious

In the concluding part of 'Champ intellectuel et projet créateur' ('The Cultural Conscious') (1969: 112) Bourdieu presented a tentative account of the unconscious process by which culture was imbibed by individuals and he speculated how this embodiment subsequently informed their actions: 'His most conscious intellectual and artistic choices are always directed by his own culture and taste, which are themselves interiorizations of the objective culture of a particular society, age or class' (Bourdieu, 1969: 112). This notion proved seminal in the crystallisation of one of Bourdieu's key analytic concepts, *habitus*, which was discussed more extensively in the Postface to his 1967 French translation of Erwin Panofsky's *Gothic Architecture and Scholasticism* (1951). However, before turning to a discussion of this text it might be appropriate to reflect on the significance of 'Champ intellectuel et project créateur'. In this one article Bourdieu outlined his three analytical concepts, field, embodiment (*habitus*) and capital. Discussion of these three concepts and their interrelations laid the foundations for the development of his general theory of practice, a project that he would pursue through numerous sociological and historical studies of cultural production over the subsequent thirty years.

Medieval scholasticism, Gothic architecture and the creative *habitus*

The research Bourdieu undertook for 'Champ intellectuel et projet créateur' included an extensive reading of the literature on art history and in particular the work of art historians who employed a historiography akin to Gaston Bachelard's exegetical method of interpreting the history of science. Bourdieu was particularly attracted to Erwin Panofsky's art-historical studies (Panofsky, 1939; 1951; 1955) which he saw as employing a method of inquiry that rejected the autonomous iconographical interpretation of art in favour of an interpretation that looked for the connection between the artist, the artistic production and the context. Some thirty years later, in a retrospective article 'The Genesis of the Concept of *Habitus* and of Field' (1985b), Bourdieu suggested that Panofsky's work helped him to crystallise his key analytical concept *habitus*, a concept he claimed allowed him to: 'break away from the structuralist paradigm without falling back into the old philosophy of the subject or of consciousness' (1985b: 13).

Bourdieu's enthusiasm for Panosfky's work led him to translate *Gothic Architecture and Scholastic Thought* (Panofsky, 1951) into French and to add a thirty-four-page Postface that provided an interpretation of Panofsky's exegesis [Bourdieu, 1967]. Bruce Holsinger has subsequently suggested that the project was 'a strangely isolated piece of Bourdieu's intellectual production' (2005: 95). However, a close reading of the Postface reveals that Bourdieu used his interpretation of Panofsky's work as a vehicle to synthesise several previously disparate strands of his thinking on the context-bound practice of creativity.

Bourdieu … ask[ed] how one might account for the correspondences between Gothic architecture and scholastic thought.

Bourdieu began the Postface by praising Panofsky's exegetical method, which he claimed went beyond the traditional art historian's concern with the identification and development of the stylistic characteristics of architecture by looking to the socio-historical context for an explanation of architectural production. In particular, Bourdieu poured scorn on the art historian Émile Mâle's interpretation of medieval creativity as the product of individual genius because, he claimed, it precluded 'discovering community at the very heart of individuality in the form of culture' (2005b: 226). Equally, he dismissed Gottfried Semper's nineteenth-century determinist notion that Gothic art was a direct expression in stone of scholastic philosophy (2005b: 229). Having rejected these interpretations Bourdieu went on to ask how one might account for the correspondences between Gothic architecture and scholastic thought. In response Bourdieu cited Panofsky's notion that the answer might lie in finding a way to discover the medieval *modus operandi*, as opposed to relying on post-facto interpretations (*modus operatum*). Clearly, Bourdieu had found synergies between Panofsky's approach and his own search, via his earlier Algerian fieldwork, for a methodology that could account for the way that people acted in real-life situations.

Panofsky's text identified certain homologies (structural similarities) between scholastic thought and Gothic architecture produced within a 100-mile radius of Paris between 1130 and 1270. He suggested that these homologies were more than mere parallelism, influence or impact, and resulted from the scholastic education system that acculturated both scholars and architects. Panofsky argued that the central tenets of scholasticism, as projected in Thomas Aquinas's authoritative text *Summa theologica*, were the notions of '*manifestatio*' (the 'postulate of clarification for clarification's sake' (Panofsky, 1951: 35)) and '*concordantia*' ('the acceptance and ultimate reconciliation of contradictory possibilities' (Panofsky, 1951: 64)). Panofsky suggested that these tenets were imbibed by medieval designers and subsequently subconsciously informed their creative acts. As a result Panofsky argued that Gothic architecture 'naturally' displayed both *manifestatio*, through its balanced formal and tectonic system of parts, their divisibility and articulation, and *concordantia*, through the harmonious co-existence of differing rule-based systems.

Panofsky named the imbibed principles that informed architects' *modus operandi* variously as a 'habit forming force', a 'mental habit', a 'habit of the mind' and 'the principle that regulates an act' (after *principium importans ordinem ad actum* from Thomas Aquinas *Summa theologica* I–II, Qtn 49, article 3, para c) and, further, suggested that 'Such mental habits are at work in all and every civilisation' (1951: 21). William Hanks has subsequently suggested that Bourdieu took Panofsky's mentalist notion and combined it with the Aristotelian notion of embodiment, or *hexis* (individual disposition that joins desire/intention with judgement/evaluation), and the phenomenological idea of habituality, or embodiment, to form the term *habitus* (derived from the Latin verb *habeo*) (Hanks, 2005: 69). Thus, Bourdieu claimed in his Postface that the term *habitus* accounted for 'the *modus operandi* capable of generating both the thoughts of the theologian and the schemes of the architect' (2005b: 233).

Bourdieu claimed ... that the term *habitus* accounted for 'the *modus operandi* capable of generating both the thoughts of the theologian and the schemes of the architect'.

Following Panofsky, Bourdieu argued that schooling produced: 'individuals endowed with this system of subconscious (or deeply buried) schemes that constitute their culture, or, better yet, their *habitus*; in short, of transforming the collective heritage into an individual and collective subconscious' (2005b: 230), and that the *habitus* provided the portal through which: 'the creator partakes of his community and time, and that guides and directs, unbeknownst to him, his apparently most unique creative acts' (2005b: 226).

Bourdieu's notion of *habitus* allowed him to account for the context-bound nature of individual cultural practice and for the existence of homologies between architecture and scholastic thought. As clarification of this point Holsinger wrote: 'Gothic architecture and scholasticism are united not only by their form of organisation and harmonisation, but in their *habitus*, the disposition that regulates the mental and bodily actions of their medieval practitioners' (2005b: 101). After explaining this seminal idea, Bourdieu then proceeded to speculate whether the notion of *habitus* could be generalised to account for the logic and existence of homologies between medieval disciplines beyond scholastic thought and Gothic architecture. Bourdieu cited Robert Marichal's twentieth-century analysis of the genesis of medieval texts, set out in *L'écriture latine et la civilisation occidentale* (Bourdieu, 2005b: 233), which described how medieval scribes developed their *habitus* through scholastic education and actualised the tenets of scholasticism on to the written page via a clarity of structure, graphic layout and letter forms (i.e. the entire system of expression) (2005b: 234–6). Bourdieu went on to suggest that a shared scholastic education could account for the striking homologies between medieval handwriting and Gothic architecture including, for example, the homology between the footing of the Gothic groined vault and the serifs of the letters in typography.

While Bourdieu's text proposed *habitus* as a conceptual tool that could account for individual creative practice, he also acknowledged the risk that the concept might be over-deterministic, akin to Noam Chomsky's notion of 'generative grammar', and might not be able to account for historical change (2005b: 233). For, as Bourdieu pointed out, the real history of architecture was characterised by periods of evolution, 'the place where the tendency to self-completion of the system of logical possibilities ... is accomplished' (2005b: 240), interspersed with periods of stylistic change or rupture. Bourdieu conceded that popularity and refinement alone could not account for stylistic ruptures, or what Thomas Kuhn had recently, in his seminal book *The Structure of Scientific Revolutions*, termed 'paradigm shifts' (Kuhn, 1962). He proceeded to point to three sources that he believed combined at certain moments in history to create aesthetic ruptures: the individual biographies of agents (that produced their *habitus*); the position of power that agents held within their respective fields, which equated with their capital; and various external exigencies that impacted on the field.

Bourdieu set out in this paradigmatic case study the central tenets of his theory of practice that were later captured in the formula: [(*habitus*) (capital)] + field = practice.

By way of an example Bourdieu suggested that the thirteenth-century victory of Abbot Suger's avant-garde aesthetics of 'light and bedazzlement' over St Bernard of Clairvaux's asceticism was the result of the confluence of three factors: first, their respective biographies (Abbot Suger was from a noble family, which pre-disposed him to excess, while St Bernard was from a poor family which pre-disposed him to restraint (2005b: 241)); second, their relative positions in society (Abbot Suger had a higher social position than St Bernard and therefore greater power to commission cultural works); and third, the shifting social context in which the two scholars worked (including rapid urbanisation, the increase of large gatherings for pilgrimages and fairs), which created demands for a new exuberant aesthetic. Thus, Bourdieu set out in this paradigmatic case study the central tenets of his theory of practice that were later captured in the formula: [(*habitus*) (capital)] + field = practice (1984a: 101).

In the concluding section of the Postface Bourdieu praised the reflexive qualities of Panofsky's methodology when he suggested that he could: 'do what he does only on condition that, at any given moment, he should know what he is doing and what it takes to be doing it' (2005b: 242).

Not long after the publication of the Postface Bourdieu turned against Panofsky, not because his work had been variously criticised for being highly selective and therefore not generally true (Holsinger, 2005: 99), but because he had decided that Panofsky's general preoccupation with iconographic interpretation led him to be 'superbly indifferent towards the question of the social conditions in which the works were produced and circulated' (Bourdieu, 1977a: 1). Yet Bourdieu's short engagement with Panofsky's *Gothic Architecture and Scholasticism* arguably proved seminal in moving him further away from both phenomenological and structuralist accounts of practice and towards a theory of practice that understood action as a result of the intersection of the individual *habitus* and the context (field). In addition Panofsky's text helped Bourdieu to develop his understanding of the powerful role educational institutions played in transforming 'the collective heritage into an individual and collective subconscious' (Bourdieu, 2005b: 230) that came to fruition three years later with the publication of *La reproduction* [Bourdieu and Passeron, 1970] (Bourdieu and Passeron, 1977).

Towards a theory of cultural practice

By the end of the 1960s Bourdieu had formulated a series of analytical concepts, *habitus*, field and capital, which he argued would help to elucidate how and why cultural producers (as social agents) acted within the field of culture (a semi-autonomous social space within the space of society) and thereby lead to a theory of cultural practice. He also declared that his new 'scientific' sociological methodology could overcome both the deterministic bias of structuralism and the subjective bias of phenomenology. However, at this stage his notion of field was still suffused with deterministic thinking. During the late 1960s and early 1970s, through a number of socio-historical and theoretical essays on literature [1971b] [1971c], art [1971d] [1974a] [1975b], education [1971g] and religion [1971e] [1971f], Bourdieu continued to exorcise the legacy of structuralism from his emerging theory of practice.

Bourdieu used Gustave Flaubert's career as a lens through which to explore the structure of the nineteenth-century literary field and its relationship with the field of power.

In the essay 'Champ du pouvoir, champ intellectuel et *habitus* de classe' ('Field of Power, Intellectual Field and Class *Habitus*') [1971b] Bourdieu extended his notion of the semi-autonomous cultural field that had previously been outlined in 'Champ intellectuel et projet créateur' ('Intellectual Field and Creative Project') [1966b] (1969) (1971a). In 'Champ du pouvoir' Bourdieu used Gustave Flaubert's career as a lens through which to explore the structure of the nineteenth-century literary field and its relationship with the field of power. He proposed, in direct opposition to Jean-Paul Sartre's biography (1991), that Flaubert had occupied a liminal (or marginal) position in social space, on the edge of both the dominant aristocratic field and the dominated field of cultural production, and that this position allowed him to objectively observe the mechanisms and interrelations between the two fields and subsequently to reify them in his novels. In 'Champ du pouvoir' Bourdieu also proposed a generic, three-stage 'scientific' method for analysing cultural practice, derived from his general sociological method outlined three years earlier in *Le métier de sociologue: Préalables épistémologiques* [Bourdieu, Chamboredon and Passeron, 1968] (Bourdieu, Chamboredon and Passeron, 1991). This method, he explained, consisted of first; 'an analysis the position of the intellectuals and artists in the structure of the ruling class/or in relation to this class'; second, 'an analysis of the structure of objective relations between the positions which the groups … occupy at any given moment in the structure of the intellectual field'; and finally, 'the constitution from these two variable contexts of the social trajectory of an individual' [1971b: 15].

In the essay 'Reproduction culturelle et reproduction sociale' ('Cultural Reproduction and Social Reproduction') [1971g] (1973b) Bourdieu returned to the theme of education. Here he transferred his generic theory of education to the cultural realm and argued that education played a 'hidden' role in reproducing the cultural *habitus* of those in power in their children, thereby ensuring the continued existence of class hierarchies.

Finally, Bourdieu's 'Le marché des biens symboliques' ('The Market of Symbolic Goods') [1971c] (1985a) (Bourdieu and Johnson, 1993: 112–41) expanded his generic 'economic' theory of capitals (social, economic and symbolic/cultural) to account for the relational positions of agents within the field of cultural production.

Relations between the field of power and the field of cultural production

Bourdieu began his essay, 'Le marché des biens symboliques', by reiterating his earlier explanation of genesis of the autonomous field of cultural production that resulted in the symbolic notion of 'art for art's sake', or 'art-as-signification', as contrasted with the utilitarian notion of 'art-as-commodity' (1971a: 164). Bourdieu then elaborated the concept of the autonomous field of cultural production by suggesting that the field was split into two parts: the field of restricted production (FRP) and the field of large-scale production (FLP), which served two different markets, each ascribing a different relative value, or capital, to the commercial and symbolic content of cultural goods. Thus, Bourdieu suggested, within the field of restricted production the economic value of a cultural product was secondary to its symbolic value and to the long-term accumulation and gestation of symbolic capital by producers and consumers alike.

Bourdieu elaborated the concept of the autonomous field of cultural production by suggesting that the field was split into two parts: the field of restricted production and the field of large-scale production.

He also suggested that the field of restricted production was the most autonomous part of the field because it was not dependent on an external market for its existence and as a consequence it had the ability to set its own beliefs and values, although these were always the subject of internal struggles. However, in contradistinction Bourdieu explained that in the field of large-scale production economic profit had primacy over symbolic value and as a result the field was orientated towards making short-term profit. Therefore, the production of goods focused on serving an immediate and large-scale market external to the field ('the public at large') and had to respond to and defer to its values.

Bourdieu clearly stated that cultural producers working in both sub-fields were highly skilled; although he also pointed out that their skills differed because they were aligned to the particularity of their respective markets. He also suggested that the field of restricted production, which included high art, or 'art for art's sake', and architecture, tended to hide its beliefs and value systems under a veil of 'idealism' and 'mystique', as a means of protectionism, whereas the field of large-scale production, which included fashion and commercial art, was altogether more open and pragmatic. However, Bourdieu warned against interpreting his notion of sub-fields as a rigid dualistic system: 'One should beware of seeing anything more than a limiting parameter construction in the opposition between the two modes of production of symbolic goods, which can only be defined in terms of their relations with each other' (1985b: 29). Yet, in 1971 Bourdieu fell short of reifying this relational model as a diagram, something he achieved a few years later in his diagrams of social space (Figures 7 and 8). As a result, in this initial exposition, his relational concept proved difficult to grasp.

In the remaining pages of the essay Bourdieu focused his attention on the field of restricted production and the way that interrelationships between producers, cultural intermediaries, institutions and consumers were mutually responsible for the production and reproduction of notions of cultural value. He began by re-asserting that cultural goods did not have intrinsic properties that made them valuable, but rather, that value was ascribed to them by those with authority (i.e. those with the most cultural capital) and, further, that those in authority were in a constant struggle to maintain their authority in the face of challenges from those who sought to take their place: 'Any act of cultural production implies an affirmation of its claim to cultural legitimacy' (Bourdieu and Johnson, 1993: 116).

Bourdieu also reminded the reader that in the field of restricted production, within which competition was primarily for cultural legitimacy, the internal economy valued culture ('symbolic' capital) over and above money ('economic' capital). Those who claimed cultural legitimacy also claimed 'distinction' because their cultural values were both 'distinct' in two senses; first, different and superior, and second, rare and therefore valuable. Bourdieu insisted that cultural values were 'arbitrarily' constructed and therefore those who claimed 'distinction' were destined to continuous challenge by newcomers to the field and aspiring cultural producers. These 'pretenders' to legitimacy produced 'novel' products, on the terms deemed legitimate by the field, as a strategy to establish new markets for their work which, if successful, would eventually lead to an increase in their cultural capital and facilitate their rise to 'distinction' and legitimacy. Drawing on Max Weber's analysis of church hierarchies, Bourdieu also asserted that those in positions of legitimacy also employed strategies, later to be termed 'symbolic violence', to maintain their position against any competition. In this respect he suggested that institutions were mechanisms used by those in dominant positions in the field to establish and delimit new or existing values, to consecrate certain cultural goods, to support certain types of cultural production over others, and to dismiss the revolutionary tendencies of the avant-garde in favour of slow evolution.

Bourdieu asserted that those in positions of legitimacy also employed strategies, later to be termed 'symbolic violence', to maintain their position against any competition.

The relation between *habitus* and field

In the final section of 'Le marché des biens symboliques' Bourdieu considered how agents' *habitus* placed them in a relational position within the field of cultural production (based on their capital volume and configuration) and then how the intersection of *habitus* and this position informed their stance, what Bourdieu called 'position-taking', which was aimed at advancing their relative position in the field. Bourdieu explained: 'intellectual or artistic position-takings are also always semi-conscious *strategies* in a game in which the conquest of cultural legitimacy and of the concomitant power of legitimate symbolic violence is at stake' (1985b: 40). In line with Bourdieu's conceptual move away from the structuralist notion of rule-based action he was keen to stress that 'position-takings' were not predetermined. Rather, he stated, 'there are an entire gamut of theoretically possible position-takings' (1985b: 35) that derived from the unconscious schemes of the *habitus*. However, Bourdieu was keen to clarify that an agent's subjective perception of the causal connection between 'position-taking' and advancement might well not take account of limitations in the objective possibilities for advancement. This, he explained, was because aspiring agents failed to recognise that those in dominant positions employed strategies, such as educational pedagogy, which presented themselves as egalitarian but were in fact designed to 'favour the favoured' (Stevens, 2002) and thereby to covertly maintain their dominance.

In 'Le marché des biens symboliques' Bourdieu set out a hypothesis that accounted for: the relations between the field of power and the field of cultural production; the relations between agents within the field of cultural production; and the actions of agents within the field. Thus, by 1971, Bourdieu had developed a tentative theory of cultural practice, a three-stage 'scientific' method, and a set of conceptual tools (*habitus*, capital and field) that prepared him for a full-scale sociological *exposé* of the ways in which culture operated in contemporary society.

CHAPTER 5

Fields of Cultural Production

By the mid-1970s Bourdieu had, through his work with Raymond Aron at the
Centre for European Sociology in Paris, helped to establish the discipline of sociology
as an autonomous academic field. He had also begun to increase his international
standing through the publication of *Esquisse d'une théorie de la pratique* in 1972
and in English, in a slightly revised form as *Outline of a Theory of Practice*, in 1977
[1972a] (1977a). Bourdieu's success allowed him to use his own, by now,
considerable cultural capital to secure funding to expand the scale and range of his
own sociological research projects and to inspire other like-minded researchers. In
1975 Bourdieu launched a new journal, *Actes de la recherche en sciences sociales*,
which aimed to provide a voice-piece for the findings of sociological investigations
into a wide range of contemporary social phenomena. In addition, Bourdieu
continued his own sociological research by exploring a number of previously
unexplored, often taboo, areas (fields) of cultural life including: sport (1978), fashion
[1974b] [Bourdieu and Desault, 1975], poetry [Bourdieu and Mammeri, 1978], taste
[Bourdieu and Saint-Martin, 1976] [Bourdieu 1979b], politics [1976] [1984b], the
housing market [Bourdieu, Christin *et al.*, 1990] [Bourdieu 2000a], television and
journalism [1996b]. These studies allowed Bourdieu to employ and refine his
scientific method, to accumulate evidence from 'cases' to further clarify his general
theory of practice, and to reveal the specific characteristics of particular fields.

Bourdieu continued his sociological research by exploring a
number of previously unexplored, often taboo, areas (fields)
of cultural life.

It is important to recognise that Bourdieu's research during the 1970s and
1980s, like his earlier Algerian fieldwork, was underpinned by political concerns.

One of his primary aims was to uncover and understand the systems of social relations (the interrelationships between individuals, fields and society) which, by being 'misrecognised', perpetuated social inequality.

This chapter discusses three of Bourdieu's field studies that related specifically to the production of material culture: fashion, literature and housing.

The field of fashion

Bourdieu published the results of his sociological foray into fashion, a relatively uncharted area of cultural production, in two articles 'Haute couture et haute culture' ('High Fashion and High Culture') [1974b] (1993: 132–8) and 'Le couturier et sa griffe: contribution à une théorie de la magie' ('The Fashion Designer and His Label: A Contribution to a Theory of Magic') [Bourdieu and Desault, 1975]. Roland Barthes had already published an important book on fashion, *The Fashion System* (1990), in 1968 that had looked at fashion through a semiotic lens. Barthes had analysed the semiotic signs within the descriptions of fashion in contemporary women's magazines and concluded that the discourse in fashion magazines created the reader's tastes in fashion which, in turn, created a market for those tastes. By contrast, Bourdieu's aim and method was firmly sociological, that is, he carried out interviews and other forms of quantitative and qualitative data collection with the aim of understanding the logic of the field of fashion.

Bourdieu's first article on the field of fashion, 'Haute couture et haute culture', was based on a lecture given in 1974 at the Noroît Cultural Centre, Arras, France, which subsequently appeared in the centre's journal. Bourdieu's second article on fashion, 'Le couturier et sa griffe: contribution à une théorie de la magie', which was jointly authored with Yves Desault, was published a year later in the first issue of *Actes de la recherche en sciences sociales* and was based on the same field data as the earlier paper. In these articles Bourdieu characterised French high fashion as a 'field of objective relations between individuals or institutions competing for the same stakes' (Bourdieu, 1993: 133) and proceeded to provide a rich description of the field as he had found it.

Bourdieu began 'Le couturier et sa griffe' by explicitly criticising Barthes's suggestion that there was a causal connection between the work of fashion journalists and the production of taste. Bourdieu claimed that Barthes's thesis was over-simplistic in that it failed to understand that there were many other agents engaged in the field of fashion (designers, buyers, shops, consumers, etc.) who were collectively involved in the production of taste. Bourdieu then proceeded to explicate this, more complex, network of relations.

Bourdieu characterised French high fashion as a 'field of objective relations between individuals or institutions competing for the same stakes'.

Fashion houses

Bourdieu hoped that his study of the field of fashion would provide a paradigmatic example of his generic theory of practice. In 'Haute couture et haute culture' he suggested that the field of fashion, like other cultural fields, existed as semi-autonomous social space within society, which contained a multiplicity of agents, who subscribed to the values of the field and its logic of operation. These agents included fashion houses who, according to Bourdieu, were positioned relationally according to the particular logic of the field, that is, according to the total volume of capital (economic + social + cultural) they possessed and the configuration of those capitals relative to the hierarchy of capitals established by the field. Bourdieu proceeded, in a very accessible way, to describe how fashion houses adopted strategies that were intended to improve their position in the field. Such strategies were based on their perceptions of the objective chances for success which, in turn, were delimited by their position in the field (their capital volume and configuration). By way of an explanation of the article's title Bourdieu defined 'haute couture' (high fashion) as the luxurious, traditional, conservative and bourgeois styles, which were produced by the most established, conservative fashion houses possessing the most capital. It was these fashion houses that occupied a dominant position in the field and adopted strategies to maintain their position. In contrast, Bourdieu identified 'haute culture' (high culture) as the 'young', inexpensive, modern, frank, intellectual styles, which were produced by new avant-garde fashion houses, who had less capital, and occupied a dominated position in the field. These 'pretenders' adopted subversive strategies that aimed to improve their standing and would, they hoped, eventually allow them to occupy the dominant position in the field. Bourdieu pointed out that it was this struggle between the pretenders and the establishment that provided the motor for change in the field (the dynamic). He also pointed out in the later article, 'Le couturier et sa griffe', that, while competition existed, all the fashion houses believed in the existence of the field of fashion; to do otherwise would be to destroy the symbolic stakes over which they competed. In other words, if the fashion houses were denied the ability to endow clothes with symbolic value the very basis on which the field was established would be destroyed and, as a result, the value of fashion would become no more than a reflection of its material value [Bourdieu and Desault, 1975: 15].

'Haute couture et haute culture' also suggested that there were uncanny homologies, or structural similarities, between the relative positions that fashion houses occupied within the social space of the field, their political leanings (left-wing or right-wing), and their location in geographical space (1993: 133–4). Thus, it followed that the left-wing avant-garde fashion houses (the pretenders who sought to unseat the established houses), including Paco Rabanne and Emanuel Ungaro, were located on Paris's 'left bank', while the conservative, consecrated fashion houses, including Christian Dior and Pierre Balmain, were located on the 'right bank'.

[Bourdieu] suggested that there were uncanny homologies … between the relative positions that fashion houses occupied within the social space of the field, their political leanings … and their location in geographical space.

Fashion designers

In 'Le couturier et sa griffe' Bourdieu suggested that fashion designers operated in a manner that was homologous to fashion houses. Thus, *haute couture* fashion designers occupied dominant positions in the field and possessed 'in the highest degree the power to define objects as rare by means of their signature, their label, those whose label has the highest price' [Bourdieu and Desault, 1975: 133].

In other words, their position in the field allowed them to bestow symbolic value on material goods and gave them seemingly alchemical powers (like Midas's ability to turn objects into gold) to turn clothes of low economic worth into clothes with high economic worth without changing their material nature. Bourdieu termed this process 'symbolic exchange': the ability to convert one kind of capital into another. Further, Bourdieu suggested that *haute couture* fashion designers cultivated the notion that they possessed magical powers of creation as a strategy to maintain their dominant positions. In contrast, Bourdieu suggested that *haute culture* fashion designers occupied dominated positions in the field because they had little cultural or economic capital and therefore they adopted avant-garde strategies (including designs) which they hoped would create successful new markets. If successful, the *haute culture* designers would see a concomitant growth in their capitals and would eventually assume the dominant position in their field (ironically representing a new form of *haute couture*). By way of an example of this *modus operandi* Bourdieu cited the way that the fashion designer André Courrèges was avante-garde in his response to the increasing freedom of women in the 1960s in his designs (he is credited, alongside Mary Quant, with inventing the mini-skirt and trouser suit), as well as in his own lifestyle:

> As for Courrèges, his apartment shows ... his revolutionary will to make a clean slate, and to rethink everything in its own terms *ex nihilo* – the spatial distribution of functions and forms, materials, and colours, all in relation to the sole imperative of comfort and effectiveness [Bourdieu and Desault, 1975: 11].

Bourdieu went on to explore the role of fashion houses in assisting the trajectory of young designers. He revealed the process by which young designers could gain legitimacy in the field by joining established houses before setting up their own fashion houses and becoming avant-garde 'pretenders'.

Bourdieu also pointed to the tension that existed within *haute couture* fashion houses between allowing junior designers the freedom of individual expression and maintaining the character of the label (a tension ever present in architectural practices). In suggesting that a founding designer's personal creativity and their socially constructed label ('griffe') were inextricably entwined Bourdieu provided a convincing account of the demise of fashion labels after the loss of their named designer (Chanel, Dior, etc). By extension, Bourdieu suggested that this truism partially accounted for the dynamic, ever-changing nature of fashion.

In the final section of the article Bourdieu considered the relationship of the field of fashion to the outside world. He suggested that designers such as Courrèges, who had the ability to assimilate external contingencies into their work, were most likely to have an upward trajectory in the field. This was because their novel products had the potential of creating new markets which would eventually replace the dominant markets; the latter being destined to go out of fashion. Bourdieu suggested that significant changes, or ruptures, within the field of fashion tended to be triggered by the external world rather than by the internal field. It followed that, as fashion houses and designers rose to orthodoxy, they were destined to become increasingly removed from the external world. As a result, both they and their work were destined to lose their dominant position to the emerging avant-garde pretenders.

Bourdieu suggested that significant changes, or ruptures, within the field of fashion tended to be triggered by the external world rather than by the internal field.

To illustrate his theory Bourdieu ended 'Le couturier et sa griffe' by suggesting that the very existence of *haute couture* was under threat because of the development of a new petit bourgeois market with novel tastes of distinction, including sport, travel, second houses, etc., and the concomitant demand for less ostentatious and more functional clothing. However, in the mid-1970s Bourdieu was not able to foresee the subsequent ability of *haute couture* to adapt to the development of new heterogeneous markets of mass consumption. Changes in the field of fashion and particularly the re-configuration of *haute couture*'s relation to the rest of the field were subsequently explored by Slater (1997: 159), Bocock (1995: 94), Varnelis (1998), Lury (1999: 81), McRobbie (1998) and Rocamora (2002a; 2002b). This work identified the increasing commercialisation of the field of fashion which led to the encroachment of commercial interests into *haute couture* (including cheaper spin-off, branded products), a burgeoning of diversity in popular fashion, and the development of a new symbiotic relationship between *haute couture* and popular fashion, all of which substantively challenged Bourdieu's dichotomous model. However, Bourdieu's later work on other sub-fields of cultural production, including art [Bourdieu, Haacke and von Inés Champey, 1994] (Bourdieu, Haacke and von Inés Champey, 1995), television and journalism [Bourdieu, 1996b] (1998d), did explore the effects of the increasing impingement of commercial interests into the field of restricted production and informed his progressive conceptual shift from structuralist to relational explanations.

The field of housing production

This section of the chapter looks at one of Bourdieu's last large-scale sociological studies, which explored the field of French housing production. In particular, the study looked at the growth of the private housing sector in late 1980s France, using the area of Val d'Oise as a case study, and involved the collection of statistical data and interviews with a variety of agents within the field: house builders, developers, house buyers, local government planners and financial lenders. The results of the study were first published in a special edition of *Actes de la recherche en sciences sociales*, entitled 'L'économie de la maison' ('The Economy of the House') [Bourdieu, Christin *et al.*, 1990], in 1990 and subsequently published as a book, *Les structures sociales de l'économie*

(The Social Structures of the Economy) [2000a] (2005a), in 2000. In the introduction to the book, Bourdieu used the findings of his case study to substantiate his generic theoretical idea that economics were a product of the social and not, as neo-liberal 'Third Way' economists claimed, a mechanism separate from, or resulting in, the social:

> **we must keep clearly in mind that the true object of a real economics of practices is nothing other, in the last analysis, than the economy of the conditions of production and reproduction of the agents and institutions of economic, cultural and social production and reproduction or, in other words, the very object of sociology in its most complete and general definition (Bourdieu, 2005a: 13).**

Further, Bourdieu called for sociologists to re-engage with the study of the economy and to position it at the heart of their discipline.

Bourdieu [posited] that economics were a product of the social and not, as neo-liberal 'Third Way' economists claimed, a mechanism separate from, or resulting in, the social.

Bourdieu presented his own case study as an *exemple par excellence* of the way that the invariant properties of fields revealed their specific forms within particular spacio-temporal settings. In the chapters that followed the Introduction Bourdieu provided a detailed discussion of the findings of his case study, which were organised into chapters that broadly aligned with his three-stage sociological method (i.e. investigate: 1 the relationship of the field to the field of politics/power; 2 the structure of the field; and 3 the actions of individual agents in the field).

Chapter 1, 'The House Market', drew on two earlier more detailed articles, 'Un placement de père de famille' [Bourdieu, Christin *et al.*, 1990: 6–33] and 'Le sens de la propriété' [Bourdieu, Christin *et al.*, 1990: 52–64]. In this chapter

Bourdieu suggested, in a similar manner to Gaston Bachelard before him (1994), that, because houses were perceived by societies as having symbolic meaning they had symbolic value as well as material, or economic, value. Therefore, the process of buying a house was perceived as a double investment: a long-term economic investment and an investment in the symbolic notion of home and family. Further, Bourdieu argued that buyers demonstrated differing preferences for housing in terms of form, content and style, which reflected their position in social space (determined by their total capital accumulation and the configuration of their capitals) and their social trajectory. The housing market duly organised itself to satisfy the complex needs of these buyers. To illustrate his thesis Bourdieu reported on the housing preferences of a newly emerging class of buyer: low-paid workers who, due to their lack of resources, had previously been in rented accommodation and possessed a 'taste for necessity'. Owing to their newly acquired access to credit, via mortgages, this new type of buyer perceived house ownership as both a financial and symbolic investment: it gave them a chance to live in their ideal 'traditional' house (2005a: 57). Bourdieu went on to describe the ways that housing developers, having identified this symbolic dimension to house-buying, used advertisements to market their houses as 'traditional', even when the 'traditional' elements were little more than *ersatz* add-ons (2005a: 58).

Bourdieu then looked in detail at the way that the sub-field of house builders was organised (2005a: 42–54). He discussed the relative social position of housing developers and builders, their past trajectories and future strategies, the struggles between firms, and the homologous relationship between firms and their markets.

Bourdieu [described] the ways that housing developers . . . used advertisements to market their houses as 'traditional', even when the 'traditional' elements were little more than *ersatz* add-ons.

Bourdieu's study gathered data from over fifty house builders and his subsequent analysis found that there were very marked differences between firms in terms of size, financial structures, manufacturing systems and marketing strategies. Such differences shaped the structure of power within the field and the way firms competed for power. For instance, Bourdieu suggested that there were large companies producing mass-manufactured housing with low symbolic value at one end of the field (FLP). This contrasted, at the other end of the field (FRP), with small businesses that supplied micro-markets, which focused mainly on producing housing using local building traditions that had a high symbolic value.

In Chapter 2, 'The State and the Construction of the Market', Bourdieu drew on 'La construction du marché' [Bourdieu, Christin et al., 1990: 65–85] to provide an explanation of the way that French government policies, emanating from the field of power, facilitated the growth of the domestic housing market. In particular, he suggested that the increasing disengagement of the government from regulating the financial markets resulted in growth, from 1966, in the mortgage market, a parallel increase in external investment in the construction industry, and a consequential decrease in the need for government housing provision for the least well-off in society. Bourdieu pointed out how, while these changes were clearly beneficial for the government and other agents involved in the production and sale of houses (house designers, house builders, material suppliers, estate agents, mortgage brokers) there was a group of agents, the working-class buyers, for whom the benefits were short-lived.

In Chapter 4 Bourdieu re-presented the earlier 'Un contrat sous contrainte' [Bourdieu, Christin et al., 1990: 34–51]. This chapter investigated the selling techniques of housing sales people and drew on real-life interactions between house buyers and sales people as well as interviews that Bourdieu carried out with each party separately. In Bourdieu's analysis of this data he revealed that sales people were aware that they were really selling credit rather than houses, and that their task was to align the aspirations of buyers with their borrowing capacity. Bourdieu's text provided disturbing descriptions of the ways that sales people used cynical marketing techniques, ranging from encouraging dreams that equated house ownership with happiness and social status to the use of a language of social familiarity and financial bafflement, to create trust:

MME F.: How did the clients around here get on in the cold snap we had a while ago?

SALESMAN: (takes advantage to *involve himself personally*) Naturally, I had no trouble with that at all. I have a G house myself (2005a: 164).

Bourdieu … provided disturbing descriptions of the ways that sales people used cynical marketing techniques … to create trust.

In the conclusions to this chapter Bourdieu included transcripts of interviews with first-time buyers that took place sometime after the purchase of their ideal homes (2005a: 185–92). He described how first-time buyers often expressed regret that they had not realised, and had not been told about, the psychological and economic costs attached to suburban isolation or the long-term debt that large mortgages entailed. When speaking about the burden of mortgage repayments, Béatrice, a forty-year-old office worker, explained: 'we didn't think about it, you're rather in cloud cuckoo land when you are buying a house. You're not really on the ball. You see the house and imagine the kids in it' (2005a: 187). Bourdieu's findings were coincidentally enacted in *Freefall*, a BBC television drama, which explored the effects of the 2009 banking crisis on ordinary people. One of the storylines described how a poor security guard was conned by an unscrupulous estate-agent friend into buying a house that was beyond his means (Savage, 2009).

Some fifteen years after its publication David Swartz and Vera Zolberg suggested that Bourdieu's seminal study illuminated the way that

the individual desire to purchase a dwelling is not simply individual but brings into play a whole range of social and political conditions that make it

> **possible or impossible. Thus housing provision is not simply a product of invisible market forces as technocratic and neo-liberal discourse would have it, but results from political decision making and political interests (Swartz and Zolberg, 2005: 346).**

Bourdieu's case study provided a convincing demonstration of his theory of the 'economy of practices', which stressed that economic factors were always integrally embedded in broad social and political phenomena.

The field of art and literature

Bourdieu's most well-known work from the 1970s was his large-scale sociological study of French taste, the results of which formed the core of *La distinction* [1979b] (1984a). It might be argued that the success of *La distinction,* initially in France and later elsewhere in Europe and America, detracted attention from his ongoing exploration of fields of cultural production. At the end of the 1970s Bourdieu also published the equally important *Le sens pratique* (*The Logic of Practice*) [1980c] (1990c), which re-worked the earlier *Esquisse d'une théorie de la pratique* [1972a] by replacing his earlier structuralist interpretations of practice (*opus operatum*) with a wholly procedural notion of practice (*modus operatum*). By the end of the 1970s, Bourdieu had decided that agents within fields adopted strategies rather than following 'objective' rules (the rules of the game) and equally, that fields were no more than the outcomes of the strategies of agents (i.e. the games were themselves strategies) (1990c: 57): 'The good player ... does at every moment what the game requires, this presupposes a permanent capacity for invention [which is] indispensable if one is to be able to adapt to infinitely varied and never completely identical situations' (1990c: 63).

Le sens pratique ... re-worked [Bourdieu's] structuralist interpretations of practice (*opus operatum*) with a wholly rocedural notion of practice (*modus operatum*).

Additionally, Bourdieu used *Le sens pratique* to outline his new belief in the 'reflexive' role of the sociological researcher, one that insisted that researchers should explicitly recognise the inescapably 'situated' nature of their position as researchers, thereby usurping his earlier notion that researchers could discover an 'objective' knowledge of the world. These conceptually significant developments underpinned Bourdieu's subsequent field studies, including those that looked at various aspects of material culture.

Throughout the 1980s Bourdieu undertook a number of socio-historical studies into the field of art and literature, which built on his earlier work on Gustave Flaubert and the socio-genesis of the nineteenth-century literary and artistic fields [1966b]. The findings of these studies were initially presented as lectures and subsequently published [1975b] (1983) (1987a) [1987b] (1988) (Bourdieu and Johnson, 1993). However, Bourdieu's major opus from the 1980s, a comprehensive sociological analysis of the nineteenth-century literary field in Paris, was *Les règles de l'art* (*The Rules of Art*) [1992] (1996a). In this text Bourdieu employed his 'scientific' sociological method, the reflexive 'three-stage analysis', to reveal how the practices of individual agents were related to the internal logic of the literary field, which was in turn related to the field of power. In many respects Bourdieu's work was the literary equivalent to Foucault's contemporaneous studies of the emergent nineteenth-century medical profession (Foucault, 2003) and penal system (Foucault, 1991). Much like *La distinction* [1979b] (1984a) before it, substantial parts of *Les règles de l'art* had been previously published and therefore the book read like a collage of disparate parts rather than a coherent narrative.

In the Preface Bourdieu suggested that his 'scientific analysis of the social conditions of the production and reception of a work of art' (1996a: xvii) was designed to challenge those who believed that art was ineffable and therefore escaped all rational understanding:

> the principle obstacle to a rigorous science of the production of value of
> cultural goods is ... [the] ... charismatic ideology which, in effect directs the
> gaze towards the apparent producer-painter, composer, writer and prevents

> us from asking who has created this 'creator' and the magic power of
> transubstantiation with which the 'creator' is endowed (1996a: 167).

He suggested that only those who owed their status to the myth of the ineffable or transcendental properties of art had anything to fear from his 'scientific' approach. However, he conceded that 'A more legitimate fear might be that science, in putting the love of art under the scalpel, might succeed in killing pleasure, and that, capable of delivering understanding, it might be unable to convey feeling' (1996a: xv–xvi). Bourdieu countered this fear by suggesting that a 'scientific' analysis would have the effect of intensifying, rather than rejecting, artistic understanding and experience (1996a: xvii). He argued that by 'feeling' the space in which the work was created, one might better understand the creator's actions. Bourdieu's new sociology of art production located creators in their own context, but avoided seeing their actions either as mere reflections of social context, as Marxist interpretations tended to do, or as the result of an autonomous disciplinary discourse, as suggested by the contemporaneous American sociologist Howard Becker and his followers (Becker, 1982).

[Bourdieu] suggested that only those who owed their status to the myth of the ineffable or transcendental properties of art had anything to fear from his 'scientific' approach.

In the Prologue to *Les règles de l'art* (1996a: 1–43) Bourdieu presented a synthesis of his earlier sociological readings of Flaubert's novel *L'Éducation sentimentale* (*Sentimental Education*): 'L'invention de la vie d'artiste' [1975a] (1987d), the three lectures given in Princeton in 1986 (Bourdieu and Johnson, 1993: 145–92) and the essay 'Flaubert's Point of View' (1988) (Bourdieu and Johnson, 1993: 192–211). Bourdieu's text suggested that Flaubert was an 'idealist' who, by dint of his liminal, or independent, social position as simultaneously inside and outside both the artistic field and the aristocratic field, was able to write reflexively. He claimed that *L'Éducation sentimentale*, a story of social relationships between characters occupying divergent social positions, provided Flaubert with a vehicle for exposing the 'hidden' structure and mechanisms of his society:

> [*Sentimental Education*] reconstitutes in an extraordinarily exact manner the structure of the social world in which it was produced and even the mental structures which, fashioned by those social structures, form the generative principle of the work in which these structures are revealed (Bourdieu, 1996a: 31–2).

Bourdieu's text commended Flaubert for having produced a literary work that spoke of serious issues in a lighthearted and digestible way and argued that the unique reflexive characteristics of Flaubert's literary work resulted from the intersection of his *habitus* and his social position within society, rather than from his innate genius. Bourdieu made two significant points in this text. First, he provided evidence to support his notion of the social construction of art and the artist. Second, he presented Flaubert as an exemplar of a 'reflexive' artist. Appendix III of the Prologue also contained an interesting map of Flaubert's Paris, which was first published in 'L'invention de la vie d'artiste'. The map attempted to show that there was a homology between the trajectory of the social positions of the main characters in *L'Éducation sentimentale* and their synchronous movement through geographical space (see Figure 9).

Bourdieu ... suggested that Flaubert was an 'idealist' who, by dint of his liminal, or independent, position ... was able to write reflexively.

As an example, the map reified Frédéric Moreau's socio-spatial trajectory. Moreau spent his student life in the bohemian Latin Quarter but, as he became progressively more established in the new bourgeois world, he moved towards the respectable fourth *arrondissement* (the business quarter). The map also charted Jacques Arnoux's downward trajectory; starting out as a businessman located in the fourth *arrondissement*, then joining the bohemian community in

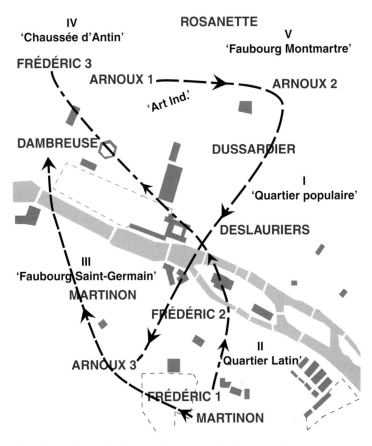

Figure 9 The Paris of *Sentimental Education*, after the map of the same name in *Les règles de l'art* [Bourdieu, 1992].

the fifth *arrondissement* (the world of art and successful artists), and finally ending up in the Latin Quarter (the world of students and failed artists) (1996a: 42).

In Part I of *Les règles de l'art*, entitled 'Three States of the Field', Bourdieu re-presented his previously published accounts [1966b] [1971c] of the history of the field of cultural production from its fifteenth-century dependence on the church and state, through the gradual emergence in the nineteenth century of an autonomous field supported by the new petite bourgeoisie, to the consolidation of the autonomous field with its own internal market for symbolic goods. Yet, somewhat surprisingly, as David Hesmondhalgh recently pointed out, Bourdieu's account failed to acknowledge late-twentieth-century developments in the field of cultural production, what Raymond Williams had termed the 'corporate professional stage' (1981), which reflected 'the growth and expansion of the cultural industries – central to which are the media industries' (Hesmondhalgh, 2006: 219). In particular, Hesmondhalgh suggested that Bourdieu's notion of the autonomous field for symbolic goods failed to either acknowledge, or account for, contemporary phenomena including: the proliferation of sub-fields in the field of restricted production (FRP); the interconnection between the field of restricted and large-scale production (FLP); and the increase of employed, as opposed to lone, cultural producers (Hesmondhalgh, 2006: 222). Given that Bourdieu acknowledged these changes in other contemporaneous publications on art (1994) and on television [1996b] his account of the field of artistic and literary production appeared disappointingly dated, perhaps the result of his reworking earlier publications.

Bourdieu set out the research methodology … which he claimed was necessary to apprehend social reality in general and the field of cultural production in particular.

In Part II, 'Foundations of a Science of Works of Art', Bourdieu set out the research methodology, his 'three-stage analytical method' [1968b], which he claimed was necessary to apprehend social reality in general and the field of cultural production in particular. He then proceeded, in Chapter 2, to present the results of his case study in the form of an analytical model of the field of cultural production that had previously appeared in 'Le marché des biens symboliques' [1971c] and in 'The Field of Cultural Production, or; The Economic World Reversed' (1983). The now-famous diagram, 'The field of cultural production in the field of power and in social space' (see Figure 10), reified all the elements of Bourdieu's conceptual model (1996a: 124). First, the base field represented 'social space' and was defined by axes indicating the possession of relative quantities of economic and cultural capital. Second, both the field of cultural production and the field of power were located in 'social space', demonstrating that the field of cultural production was a dominated fraction of the dominant class. Finally, the field of cultural production was itself split into two fractions, the field of small-scale, or 'restricted' production (FRP), and the field of large-scale production (FLP), and artists were positioned relationally according to their capital.

Bourdieu's text explained that those artists in the field of small-scale production had a high degree of autonomy and produced 'art for art's sake' or 'production for producers' and further, that successful artists were likely to reap high symbolic rewards in the short term and potentially high economic rewards in the long term. By contrast, artists in the field of large-scale production were tied to meeting the immediate demands of external markets and as a result their short-term economic profits were often high. However, the symbolic rewards for artists in the field of large-scale production were low and, as a result, their

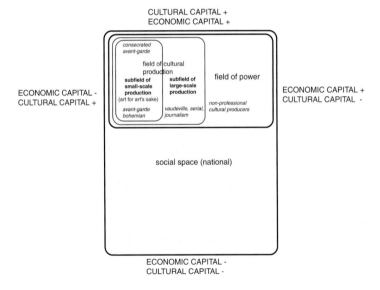

Figure 10 The field of cultural production in the field of power and in social space, after the diagram of the same name in *Les règles de l'art* [Bourdieu, 1992].

long-term economic profits were also likely to be low because their work would never be consecrated (Bourdieu, 1996a: 142–3).

While the clarity of Bourdieu's diagram proved attractive, arguably its clarity was also its downfall. The diagram failed to overcome the problem of representing how the field changed over time, a difficulty identified by Bourdieu himself in relation to both his Algerian work (1990c: 81) and his mapping of social space (1984a: 128–9). Bourdieu's accompanying narrative attempted to ameliorate this problem by stressing that the field only existed as the sum of the 'position-takings' (stances) of individual agents within the field and that these 'position-takings' were constantly changing. Bourdieu's conceptual diagram was also criticised for its failure to recognise both the fuzziness of field boundaries (Swartz, 1997: 132) and the possibility that agents might exist in multiple fields at any one moment in time (Bennett *et al.*, 2009: 172). Bourdieu's diagram also deployed the questionable methodological assumption, inherited from *Distinction*, that material 'economic capital' and metaphorical 'cultural capital' had an objective equivalence (Frow, 1995: 39–40). In addition, Bourdieu's notion of the dichotomous relationship between the field of small-scale production and large-scale production appeared to belie his conceptual shift away from structuralism and towards relational thinking. Consequentially, in the final reckoning Bourdieu's enigmatic diagram of the field of cultural production appeared to raise more questions than it answered.

Bourdieu's notion of the dichotomous relationship between the field of small-scale production and large-scale production appeared to belie his conceptual shift away from structuralism and towards relational thinking.

In Part III, 'To Understand Understanding', Bourdieu returned to two earlier themes: the historically constituted nature of aesthetic dispositions, and the role education played in restricting access to the acquisition of legitimised aesthetic dispositions. These were originally discussed in 'Éléments d'une théorie sociologique de la perception artistique' [1968b] and *L'amour de l'art: les musées d'art européens et leur public* [Bourdieu, Darbel and Schnapper, 1966]. Bourdieu was keen to restate the notion that the meaning of cultural artefacts was not embodied in the object, but rather, was made afresh by each viewer. Therefore, to understand the meaning that a work of art held for the original artist, or for the subsequent viewer, one had to perform the task of re-constructing a model of the codes that tacitly informed individual creative acts and interpretative practices (1996a: 314–15). Interestingly, some twenty-four years after the publication of 'Éléments d'une théorie sociologique de la perception artistique' Bourdieu finally managed to abandon the language of structuralism to explain aesthetic perception and practice, replacing it with a procedural language that could account for the tacit nature of practice. He wrote:

> **The science of the mode of aesthetic knowledge finds its foundation in a theory of practice as practice, meaning as an activity founded in cognitive operations which mobilize a mode of knowing which is not that of theory and concept, without nevertheless being … a sort of ineffable participation in a known object (1996a: 315).**

Bourdieu concluded Part III by suggesting that, while cultural perception appeared to be the result of some inexplicable 'sense' or 'feeling' it was in fact the result of the subconscious decoding and reasoning of the 'learned' *habitus* (1996a: 320). He claimed that if researchers were to begin to understand individual art reception or creation they had to immerse themselves in the historical particularity of a place and time of the viewing or making.

Bourdieu [suggested] that, while cultural perception appeared to be a result of some inexplicable 'sense' or 'feeling' it was in fact the result of the subconscious decoding and reasoning of the 'learned' *habitus*.

Critics of *Les règles de l'art* suggested that this work, like *La distinction* before it, neglected both the form and the power of popular culture and failed to recognise the increasing influence of the media and cultural industries (Hesmondhalgh, 2006: 217–23). In Bourdieu's defence, much of his text drew upon research on the nineteenth-century literary field that was carried out between the 1963 and the mid-1980s, which pre-dated the rise of the culture industries and the burgeoning of popular cultures. Further, Bourdieu did explicitly address the contemporary condition in the 'new' Postscript, 'For a Corporatism of the Universal' (1996a: 337–48), that appeared at the end of the book. In this short, but impassioned text, Bourdieu railed against modern-day commercial interests, in the form of the culture industries, which, he claimed, impinged on the autonomy of intellectual life and as a result made it increasingly difficult for intellectuals to act as disinterested moral and ethical critics of society. Rather than considering popular culture as the locale for subversion, revolt and radical change, as cultural theorists were attempting to do at the time, Bourdieu considered that the autonomous intellectual field, his own field, was the only place where work that was truly critical of the neo-liberal system, and particularly the social inequalities it produced, could be generated. Thus, he called for intellectuals to stand together to defend their autonomy in order to ensure the continued existence of a group who could act as the conscience of society. Arguably, the Postscript was the only section of *Les règles de l'art* that truly reflected Bourdieu's latest intellectual commitment.

CHAPTER 6

Cultural Practice, Reflexivity and Political Action

Bourdieu became associated with overt public political protest in the last decade of his life, which marked a remarkable change in his *modus operandi*. It is of course arguable that his prior sociological practice, which focused on uncovering the social conditions of the oppressed was, from the earliest days, implicitly political. Over the course of forty years of practice, Bourdieu's research engaged with many different social 'crises': the Algerian oppression under colonialism in the 1950s; the student revolts against state education policies in the 1960s; the plight of the poor; the erosion of the welfare state; and the autonomy of cultural producers under neo-liberalism. While his methods of practice changed, from anthropology to sociology and finally to political action, much of his work attempted to reveal the powerful 'hidden' mechanisms that perpetuated an unequal world and he never ceased to believe that his contribution was a pre-requisite to social reform.

'If there is a truth, it is that truth is a stake in the struggle'

(Bourdieu and Johnson, 1993: 263).

In a sense, Bourdieu's career might be understood as a journey during which he continuously refined both his notion of why cultural practice was inescapably political and, through his own practice, how cultural practice could lead to social reform. For most of his career, as the preceding chapters attest, Bourdieu worked from his position in the sociological field to unravel the logic of other important cultural fields including: religion, education, art, literature, fashion and sport. His research produced some penetratingly critical *exposés* of cultural fields [1975a] [1984c] [1992] [2000a], a general, ever-evolving, theory of practice [1972a] [1980c] [2000a], and a new sociological method – which he termed 'reflexive' sociology [1968b] [1987e] [1992] [2001b]. For Bourdieu 'reflexivity' offered a way for researchers to explicitly recognise (or declare) that their perspectives on the objects of their research were inescapably derived from their own contemporary position in the field of sociology. Bourdieu's notion of reflexivity began as a precept of his sociological method. However, through his studies of Gustave Flaubert's novels (1987d), Édouard Manet's paintings (Bourdieu and Johnson, 1993: 236–53) and Émile Zola's political activism (1996a: 341–2), Bourdieu came to believe that reflexivity was a necessary prerequisite for all cultural producers (writers, artists, intellectuals, etc.) if their thoughts and actions were to escape from being unknowingly bounded by the arbitrary logic of their respective fields. Further, Bourdieu claimed that reflexive practice could 'promote struggles aimed at controlling these effects and the mechanisms that produce them' (Swartz, 1997: 271).

During the 1990s, the last decade of Bourdieu's life, he became increasingly concerned about the deleterious effects of neo-liberalism including: the erosion of the welfare state, the worsening conditions of the poor, the commercialisation of the media, and the erosion of academic and artistic freedom. In response Bourdieu began to use his personal status as Chair of Sociology at the Collège de France (1982–2001) in the political arena to bring these issues to public awareness and to support progressive groups (unions, gay lobbies, etc.) through overtly political speeches, talks, television appearances [L'Hôte, 1996] and protests. Derek Robbins, one of the leading academic commentators on Bourdieu's work has suggested that, during the 1990s, Bourdieu transformed his personal social position from being a sociologist looking objectively at culture to a cultural figure who used his cultural and social capital, and his relative autonomy, for explicitly political purposes (2000b: xxv). Somewhat ironically Bourdieu ended his career by using his capital, and the power that went with it, against the very system that was its source. In many respects Bourdieu's publications from this period, including *Contre-feux* (*Acts of Resistance: Against the New Myths of our Time*) [1998c] (1998b), *Contre-feux 2* (*Firing Back: Against the Tyranny of the Market 2*) [2001a] (2003a), *Sur la télévision* [1996b] and *La misère du monde* [Bourdieu and Accardo, 1993], represented his most publicly accessible work.

Bourdieu ended his career by using his capital, and the power that went with it, against the very system that was its source.

Although Bourdieu spent much of the 1990s addressing new audiences, he also continued his discourse with cultural practitioners. As early as 1989 Bourdieu had published a paper, 'The Corporatism of the Universal' (1989), which outlined his perception of external threats to the autonomy of the cultural field. These included: the increasing encroachment of the state and penetration of economic interest into the world of art and science; the consolidation of large bureaucracies that managed television, radio and the press into an establishment that imposed its own standards of production and consumption; and the related tendency to strip intellectuals of their ability to evaluate themselves, substituting instead the journalistic criteria of topicality, readability and novelty. Bourdieu went on to elaborate his diagnosis and to challenge cultural practitioners to: first, recognise their condition, through reflexivity; second, fight to regain their autonomy; third, use their autonomy to frame a critique of neo-liberalism and to design a new utopian alternative.

At the end of *Les règles de l'art* (1996a: 337–48), Bourdieu explicitly argued that neo-liberalism was illicitly eroding autonomy of the cultural field and thereby the capacity of cultural practitioners to act freely as critics and reformers, and he called on cultural practitioners to group together to regain their autonomy and mount an effective critique of neo-liberalism.

In a conversation between Bourdieu and the artist Hans Haacke, which was subsequently published in 1994 as *Libre-Échange* (*Free Exchange*) [Bourdieu, Haacke and von Inés Champey, 1994] (Bourdieu, Haacke and von Inés Champey, 1995), Bourdieu outlined the ways contemporary artists were 'compromised' by such things as the dependency and restrictions that resulted from the commercial and state funding of art, and the power of the media to censor the dissemination of art. He suggested that by acting out of self-interest, by either colluding with the commercialised field of artistic production or by pretending that they worked according to higher ideals, contemporary artists were in denial of their complicity with the processes that were gradually eroding their hard-won autonomy. Yet in the same book Bourdieu cited the work of the same German artist, Hans Haacke, including his controversial 1990 Berlin watchtower topped with a Mercedes Benz star (Bourdieu, Haacke and von Inés Champey, 1995: 94), as an example of the way artists could, through reflexivity, understand their own condition and then, from that position of freedom, produce politically charged work.

Bourdieu argued that it was the duty of cultural practitioners to resist the ills of neo-liberalism.

Bourdieu, following his understanding of Émile Zola's actions during the Dreyfus Affair (1996a: 342), resolutely championed the 'political artist' and attacked those who acted as 'artist politicians'. Bourdieu also attacked writers, journalists and those involved in the creation of television programmes (1998b: 70–7) (1998d) (Bourdieu, Poupeau and Discepolo, 2008: 321–3; 333–9) for their complicity with the commercialism and conservatism of the media and challenged them to adopt a reflexive stance.

In *Contre-feux* [1998c] Bourdieu argued that it was the duty of cultural practitioners to resist the ills of neo-liberalism: 'Artists, writers and researchers (including sociologists) have the capacity, and the duty, to combat the most malign of the threats that this global production implies for culture and democracy' (1998b: 77). He also called on cultural practitioners to engage more directly in the political arena:

> **I would like writers, artists, philosophers and scientists to be able to make their voice heard directly in all areas of public life in which they are**

competent. I think that everyone would have a lot to gain if the logic of intellectual life, that of argument and refutation, were extended to public life (1998b: 9).

Bourdieu's plea to intellectuals went further than asking them to mobilise in resistance to neo-liberalism. In his acceptance speech for the Bloch Prize in 1997 Bourdieu argued that intellectuals had a duty to work towards a 'reasoned utopianism', an extrapolation of Ernst Bloch's notion of the 'considered utopian', that might challenge the dominant ideology of the age, which he characterised as 'the bankers' fatalism' (1998a: 128). During the lecture he advocated that 'intellectuals, and all others who really care about the good of humanity, should re-establish a utopian thought with scientific backing' (Bourdieu, 1998a: 128).

Although Bourdieu rejected modernist notions of objective truths when he proposed his relativist model of society and practice, which in many ways aligned with post-modernism, he maintained a belief in the rational search for universally agreed humanist principles. He worried that the abandonment of modernist values would result in a return to conservatism and thereby open the door to unfettered commercialism. Bourdieu argued that collective international action was needed to resist the global forces of neo-liberalism. In a talk given in June 2000 at the Centre Beaubourg in memory of Michel Foucault he insisted that the intellectual collective 'will have to invent a way of organising the collective work of producing realistic utopias and inventing new forms of symbolic action' (Bourdieu, 2008: 387). To this end he attempted to rally cultural practitioners through numerous articles and books, and by creating international publications and organisations, including his own journal *Liber*, a European review of books (1989–98) and a publishing house, Raisons d'agir, that provided an autonomous space, free from the controls of either state or commercial interests, for artists and scientists to debate. He also worked tirelessly to bring like-minded people to together, including trade unions, gay-rights groups, advocates for the rights of the homeless, and anti-racism associations, through formal groups such as the International Parliament of Writers (founded 1993), the Association for Rethinking Higher Education and

Research (Areser), and the General Estates of the European Social Movement. These groups, all of which are still extant, represented real manifestations of Bourdieu's notion of the 'intellectual collective', although his notion of a 'reasoned utopia' remains ill defined. Pierre Carles's film *Sociologie est un sport combat (Sociology is a Martial Art)* [2001] (2002), which followed Bourdieu over a period of three years, from 1998 to 2001, as he carried out a whole range of engagements including attending protests, lecturing to students and discussing his work with his colleagues, demonstrated the modesty, passion and energy that he put into challenging neo-liberalism. Sadly, Bourdieu died of cancer in 2002 leaving others to continue his work.

Pierre Carles's film *Sociologie est un sport combat* ...

demonstrated the modesty, passion and energy that

[Bourdieu] put into challenging neo-liberalism.

At the end of *Pierre Bourdieu: Esquisse pour une auto-analyse (Pierre Bourdieu: Sketch for Self-Analysis)* [2004b] (2007a), which he insisted was 'not an autobiography', Bourdieu suggested that he wrote the book to provide readers with information that would help them to understand the 'historical conditions in which my work was developed' (2007a: 112). Just as Bourdieu hoped to understand the actions of cultural practitioners, be it Flaubert, Manet or Zola, through his reflexive methodology, he hoped that readers would use the same methodology to explore his own work and in doing so they might:

> recognise their own experiences, difficulties, questionings, sufferings, and so on, in mine, and to draw from that realistic identification, which is quite the opposite of exalted projection, some means of doing what they do, and living what they live, a little better (2007a: 113).

In an era in which architects increasingly perceive their role as being limited to serving the, often banal, demands of those who profit from neo-liberalism (Dubai might be considered an example *par excellence* of this phenomenon),

Bourdieu's call for cultural producers to start fighting for a better world for all seems both relevant and pressing. Ultimately, this book aims to inspire architects to respond to Pierre Bourdieu's rallying cry by 'reflexively' recognising the conditions of their own position in society and subsequently to play their part in the formulation and realisation of a 'reasoned utopia'.

Further Reading

The burgeoning literature on Pierre Bourdieu views his work through various disciplinary lenses including anthropology, sociology, art history, cultural studies, geography and philosophy. Derek Robbins' books on Bourdieu (1991; 2000a; 2000b; 2005), and particularly *The Work of Pierre Bourdieu: Recognising Society* (1991) and *Bourdieu and Culture* (2000), provide a comprehensive and accessible overview of Bourdieu's work. Bridget Fowler has also published extensively on Bourdieu and culture (1994; 1997; 1999). In addition, there are several fascinating sociological studies that both apply and extend Bourdieu's work on material culture including: Michael Grenfell and Cheryl Hardy's study of art, museums and photography, *Art Rules: Pierre Bourdieu and the Visual Arts* (2007); Tony Bennett, Michael Emmison and John Frow's study of Australian taste, *Accounting for Taste: Aesthetics of Everyday Cultures* (1999); and Tony Bennett *et al.*'s study of British taste, *Culture, Class, Distinction* (2009). For literature that relates Bourdieu's ideas to the field of architecture one might look at: Gary Stevens' book on architectural education, *The Favoured Circle: The Social Foundations of Architectural Distinction* (2002); Jean Hillier and Eric Rookesby's book of edited essays on place and meaning, *Habitus: A Sense of Place* (2005); Michel de Certeau's seminal work on agency and the city, *The Practice of Everyday Life* (1984); and Hélène Lipstadt's articles that relate Bourdieu's work to the architecture profession (2000; 2001; 2003; 2004).

A comprehensive bibliography and mediagraphy of all works by Bourdieu can be found in the *Hyper Bourdieu World Catalogue.*

Finally, as this book makes clear, the French-language editions of Bourdieu's texts are the basic and indispensible source for further study. The French editions of Bourdieu's work often contain substantial amounts of text and empirical data that were subsequently omitted from the English translations. In addition, the graphic quality of the texts powerfully evokes the period in which they were published and, as such, help the reader to understand that they are inextricably linked to their socio-historical context.

Bibliography

Knowledge of the chronology of Bourdieu's texts is critical for understanding the development of his ideas, so the bibliography below provides details for the publication of a text both in French (in square brackets) and in English (in parentheses).

Selected texts by Pierre Bourdieu

Bourdieu, P. [1958] (1962b) *Sociologie de l'Algérie,* Paris: Presses universitaires de France.

—— [1959a] 'Logique interne de la civilisation algérienne traditionnelle', in *Le sous-développement en Algérie*, Algiers: Secrétariat social, pp. 40–51.

—— [1959b] 'Le choc des civilisations', in *Le sous-développement en Algérie*, Algiers: Secrétariat social, pp. 52–64.

—— [1960a] *Deux essais sur la société kabyle: Le sentiment de l'honneur dans la société kabyle; La maison kabyle ou le monde renversé,* Paris: Publication ronéotypée.

—— [1960b] 'Guerre et mutation sociale en Algérie', *Études méditerranéennes* 7, 25–37.

—— [1962a] 'Célibat et condition paysanne', *Études rurales* 5–6, 32–136.

—— (1962b) [1958] *The Algerians,* translated by A. C. M. Ross, Boston, MA: Beacon Press.

—— (1963) 'The Attitude of the Algerian Peasant towards Time', in J. Pitt-Rivers (ed.) *Mediterranean Countrymen*, Paris: Mouton, pp. 55–72.

—— (1965) [1960a] [1972a: 13–43] 'The Sentiment of Honour in Kabyle Society', in J. G. Peristiany (ed.) *Honour and Shame. The Values of Mediterranean Society*, London: Weidenfeld and Nicholson, pp. 191–241.

—— [1966a] (1969) (1971a) 'Champ intellectuel et projet créateur', *Les temps modernes* 22, 865–906.

—— [1966b] 'Condition de classe et position de classe', *Archives européennes de sociologie* 7.2, 201–23.

—— [1967] (2005b) 'Postface', in E. Panofsky, *Architecture gothique et pensée scolastique*, translated by P. Bourdieu, Paris: Éditions de Minuit, pp. 133–67.

—— (1968a) [1968b] (Bourdieu and Johnson, 1993: 215–37) 'Outline of a Sociological Theory of Art Perception', *International Social Science Journal* 2.4, 589–612.

—— [1968b] (1968a) (Bourdieu and Johnson, 1993: 215–37) 'Éléments d'une théorie sociologique de la perception artistique', *Revue internationale des sciences sociales* 20.4, 640–64.

—— (1969) (1971a) [1966a] 'Intellectual Field and Creative Project', *Social Science Information* 8.2, 89–119.

—— (1970a) [1970b] 'The Berber House or the World Reversed', *Social Science Information* 9.2, 151–70.

—— [1970b] (1970a) 'La maison Kabyle ou le monde renversé', in J. Pouillon and P. Maranda (eds) *Échanges et communications: Mélanges offerts à Claude Lévi-Strauss à l'occasion de son 60ème anniversaire*, Paris, The Hague: Mouton, pp. 739–58.

—— (1971a) [1966a] (1969) 'Intellectual Field and Creative Project', in M. F. D. Young (ed.) *Knowledge and Control: New Directions in the Sociology of Education*, London: Collier-Macmillan, pp. 161–88.

—— [1971b] 'Champ du pouvoir, champ intellectuel et *habitus* de classe', *Scolies: Cahiers de recherches de l'École normale supérieure* 1, 7–26.

—— [1971c] (1985a) 'Le marché des biens symboliques', *L'année sociologique* 22, 49–126.

—— [1971d] (1994) 'Disposition esthétique et compétence artistique', *Les temps modernes* 27, 1345–78.

—— [1971e] (1987c) 'Une interprétation de la théorie de la religion selon Max Weber', *Archives européennes de sociologie* 12.1, 3–21.

—— [1971f] (1991a) 'Genèse et structure du champ religieux', *Revue française de sociologie* 12.3, 295–334.

—— [1971g] (1973b) 'Reproduction culturelle et reproduction sociale', *Information sur les sciences sociales* 10.2, 45–79.

—— [1972a] (1977a) *Esquisse d'une théorie de la pratique: Précédé de trois études d'ethnologie kabyle*, Geneva and Paris: Librairie Droz.

—— [1972b] 'Les doxosophes', *Minuit* 1, November, 26–45.

—— (1973a) 'The Berber House', in M. Douglas (ed.) *Rules and Meanings*, Harmondsworth: Penguin, pp. 98–110.

—— (1973b) [1971g] 'Cultural Reproduction and Social Reproduction', in R. Brown (ed.) *Knowledge, Education and Cultural Change*, London: Tavistock, pp. 71–112.

—— [1974a] 'Les fractions de la classe dominante et les modes d'appropriation des œuvres d'art', *Information sur les sciences sociales* 13.3, 7–31.

—— [1974b] [1980b: 196–206] (1993: 132–8) 'Haute couture et haute culture', *Noroît* 192.1–2, 7–17.

—— [1975a] (1987d) 'L'invention de la vie d'artiste', *Actes de la recherche en sciences sociales* 1.2, 67–93.

—— [1975b] 'Méthode scientifique et hiérarchie sociale des objets', *Actes de la recherche en sciences sociales* 1.1, 4–6.

—— [1976] (1984a: 546–59) 'Un jeu chinois: notes pour une critique sociale du jugement', *Actes de la recherche en sciences sociales* 4.10, 91–101.

—— (1977a) [1972a] *Outline of a Theory of Practice*, translated by R. Nice, Cambridge, UK: Cambridge University Press.

—— [1977b] (1979a) *Algérie soixante: Structures économiques et structures temporelles*, Paris: Éditions de Minuit.

—— [1977c] (1980a) La production de a croyance. Contribution à une économie des biens symboliques', *Actes de la recherche en science sociales* 3, 3–43.

—— (1978) 'Sport and Social Class', *Social Science Information* 17.6, 810–40.

—— (1979a) [1977b] *Algeria 1960: Essays by Pierre Bourdieu*, translated by R. Nice, Cambridge, UK: Cambridge University Press.

—— [1979b] (1984a) *La distinction: critique sociale du jugement*, Paris: Éditions de Minuit.

—— (1980a) [1977c] (Bourdieu and Johnson, 1993: 74–111) 'The Production of Belief: Contribution to an Economy of Symbolic Goods', translated by R. Nice, *Media, Culture and Society* 2.3, 261–93.

—— [1980b] (1993) *Questions de sociologie,* Paris: Éditions de Minuit.

—— [1980c] (1990c) *Le sens pratique*, Paris: Éditions de Minuit.

—— (1983) (Bourdieu and Johnson, 1993: 29–73) 'The Field of Cultural Production, or: The Economic World Reversed', *Poetics* 12.4–5, 311–56.

—— (1984a) [1979b] *Distinction: A Social Critique of the Judgement of Taste*, translated by R. Nice, Oxford: Polity Press.

—— [1984b] (1985c) 'La délégation et le fétichisme politique', *Actes de la recherche en sciences sociales* 52–3, June, 49–55.

—— [1984c] (1990b) *Homo academicus*, Paris: Éditions de Minuit.

—— (1985a) [1971c] 'The Market of Symbolic Goods', *Poetics: Journal of Empirical Research on Literature, the Media and the Arts* 14.1–2, 13–44.

—— (1985b) 'The Genesis of the Concept of *Habitus* and of Field', *Sociocriticism* 2.2, 11–24.

—— (1985c) [1984b] 'Delegation and Political Fetishism', *Thesis Eleven* 10/11, 56–70.

—— (1986) 'The Struggle for Symbolic Order' (a discussion between P. Bourdieu, A. Honneth, H. Kocyba and P. B. Schwibs), *Theory, Culture and Society* 3.3, 37–51.

—— (1987a) (Bourdieu and Johnson, 1993) 'The Historical Genesis of a Pure Aesthetic', *Journal of Aesthetics and Art Criticism* 46, special issue, 201–10.

—— [1987b] (Bourdieu and Johnson, 1993: 238–53) 'L'institutionnalisation de l'anomie', *Cahiers du Musée national d'art moderne* 19–20, June, 6–19.

—— (1987c) [1971e] 'Legitimation and Structured Interests in Weber's Sociology of Religion', in S. Whimster and S. Lash (eds) *Max Weber: Rationality and Modernity*, London: Allen and Unwin, pp. 119–36.

—— (1987d) [1975a] 'The Invention of the Artist's Life', *Yale French Studies* 73, 75–103.

—— [1987e] (1990a) *Choses dites*, Paris: Éditions de Minuit.

—— (1988) (Bourdieu and Johnson, 1993: 192–211) 'Flaubert's Point of View', translated by P. Parkhurst Ferguson, *Critical Enquiry* 14.3, 539–62.

—— (1989) 'The Corporatism of the Universal: The Role of Intellectuals in the Modern World', *Telos* 81, Fall, 99–110.

—— (1990a) [1987e] *In Other Words: Essays towards a Reflexive Sociology*, translated by M. Adamson, Stanford, CA: Stanford University Press.

—— (1990b) [1984c] *Homo Academicus*, translated by P. Collier, Cambridge, UK: Polity Press.

—— (1990c) [1980c] *The Logic of Practice*, translated by R. Nice, Oxford: Polity Press.

—— (1991a) [1971f] 'Genesis and Structure of the Religious Field', *Comparative Social Research* 13, 1–44.

—— (1991b) 'Social Space and Symbolic Space: Introduction to a Japanese Reading of *Distinction*', *Poetics Today* 12.4, 627–38.

—— [1992] (1996a) *Les règles de l'art: Genèse et structure du champ littéraire*, Paris: Éditions du Seuil.

—— (1993) [1980b] *Sociology in Question*, translated by R. Nice, London: Sage.

—— (1994) 'The Link between Literary and Artistic Struggles', in P. Collier and R. Lethbridge (eds) *Artistic Relations: Literature and the Visual Arts in Nineteenth-Century France*, New Haven: Yale University Press, pp. 30–9.

—— (1996a) [1992] *The Rules of Art: Genesis and Structure of the Literary Field*, translated by S. Emanuel, Oxford: Polity Press.

—— [1996b] (1998d) *Sur la télévision*, Paris: Éditions Liber.

—— [1997] (1999) *Méditations pascaliennes: Éléments pour une philosophie négative*, Paris: Éditions du Seuil.

—— (1998a) 'A Reasoned Utopia and Economic Fatalism', translated by J. Howe, *New Left Review* 227, January–February, 125–30.

—— (1998b) [1998c] *Acts of Resistance: Against the New Myths of Our Time*, translated by R. Nice, Oxford: Polity Press.

—— [1998c] (1998b) *Contre-feux: Propos pour servir à la résistance contre l'invasion néo-libérale*, Paris: Éditions Liber.

—— (1998d) [1996b] *On Television*, translated by P. Parkhurst Ferguson, New York: The New Press.

—— (1999) [1997] *Pascalian Meditations*, translated by R. Nice, Stanford, CA: Stanford University Press.

—— [2000a] (2005a) *Les structures sociales de l'économie*, Paris: Collection Liber, Éditions du Seuil.

—— (2000b) 'The Berber House – A World Reversed', in J. Thomas (ed.) *Interpretive Archaeology: A Reader*, London and New York: Leicester University Press, pp. 493–509.

—— [2001a] (2003a) *Contre-feux 2: Pour un mouvement social européen,* Paris: Éditions Raisons d'agir.

—— [2001b] (2004a) *Science de la science et réflexivité*, Paris: Éditions Raisons d'agir.

—— [2002] (2008) *Interventions politiques (1961–2001): Textes et contextes d'un mode d'intervention politique spécifique*, Marseille: Éditions Agone; Montreal: Comeau and Nadeau.

—— (2003a) [2001a] *Firing Back: Against the Tyranny of the Market* 2, translated by L. Wacquant, New York, London: The New Press.

—— [2003b] 'In Algier und Bilda', in F. Schultheis and C. Frisinghelli (eds) *Images d'Algérie: Une affinité élective,* Graz: Edition Camera Austria, pp. 191–216.

—— (2003c) 'The Berber House', in S. M. Low and D. Lawrence-Zúñiga (eds), *The Anthropology of Place and Space*, Oxford: Blackwell Publishing, pp. 131–41.

—— (2004a) [2001b] *Science of Science and Reflexivity*, translated by R. Nice, London: Polity.

—— [2004b] (2007a) *Pierre Bourdieu: Esquisse pour une auto-analyse*, Paris: Éditions Raisons d'agir.

—— (2004c) 'Algerian Landing', translated by L. Wacquant and R. Nice, *Ethnography* 5.4, 415–43.

—— (2005a) [2000a] *The Social Structures of the Economy*, translated by C. Turner, Cambridge, UK: Polity Press.

—— (2005b) [1967] 'Postface to Erwin Panofsky, *Gothic Architecture and Scholasticism*', translated by L. Petit, in B. Holsinger, *The Premodern Condition*, London and Chicago: University of Chicago Press, pp. 221–42.

—— (2007a) [2004b] *Pierre Bourdieu: Sketch for a Self-Analysis*, translated by R. Nice, Cambridge, UK: Polity Press.

—— (2007b) 'Pictures from Algeria', translated by R. Watts, *Sociology*, March, pp. 22–27.

—— (2008) [2002] *Political Interventions: Social Science and Political Action*, translated by D. Fernbach, London: Verso.

Bourdieu, P. and A. Accardo (eds) [1993] (1999) *La misère du monde*, Paris: Éditions du Seuil.

—— (eds) (1999) [1993] *The Weight of the World*: *Social Suffering in Contemporary Society*, translated by P. Parkhurst Ferguson, S. Emanuel, J. Johnson and T. Waryn, Cambridge, UK: Polity Press.

Bourdieu, P., L. Boltanski, R. Castel, J.-C. Chamboredon, G. Lagneau and
D. Schnapper [1965] (1989) *Un art moyen, essai sur les usages sociaux de la
photographie*, Paris: Éditions de Minuit.

—— (1989) [1965] *Photography: A Middle-brow Art*, translated by S. Whiteside,
Cambridge, UK: Polity Press.

Bourdieu, P. and M.-C. Bourdieu [1965] (2004) 'Le paysan et la photographie',
Revue française de sociologie 6.2, 164–74.

—— (2004) [1965] 'The Peasant and Photography', translated by R. Nice,
Ethnography 5.4, 601–16.

Bourdieu, P., J.-C. Chamboredon and J.-C. Passeron [1968] (1991) *Le métier de
sociologue: Préalables épistémologiques*, Paris: Mouton and Bordas.

—— (1991) [1968] *The Craft of Sociology: Epistemological Preliminaries*,
translated by R. Nice, New York and Berlin: de Gruyter.

Bourdieu, P., R. Christin, S. Bouhedia, C. Givry and M. de Saint-Martin [1990]
'L'économie de la maison', *Actes de la recherche en sciences sociales* 81–2,
March, 2–96.

Bourdieu, P., A. Darbel, J.-P. Rivet and C. Seibel [1963] *Travail et travailleurs en
Algérie,* Paris: Éditions de Minuit.

Bourdieu, P., A. Darbel and D. Schnapper [1966] (1990) *L'amour de l'art: Les
musées d'art européens et leur public*, Paris: Éditions de Minuit.

—— (1990) [1966] *The Love of Art: European Art Museums and Their Public*,
translated by C. Beattie and N. Merriman, Cambridge, UK: Polity Press.

Bourdieu, P. and Y. Desault [1975] 'Le couturier et sa griffe: contribution à une
théorie de la magie', *Actes de la recherche en sciences sociales* 1.1,
7–36.

Bourdieu, P., H. Haacke and V. von Inés Champey [1994] (1995) *Libre-Échange*,
Paris: Éditions du Seuil.

—— (1995) [1994] *Free Exchange*, translated by R. Johnson, Cambridge, UK:
Polity Press in association with Blackwell Publishing.

Bourdieu, P. and R. Johnson (ed.) (1993) *The Field of Cultural Production: Essays
on Art and Literature*, translated by R. Nice, R. Swyer, C. Du Verlie,
P. Parkhurst and J. Parnell, Oxford: Polity Press.

Bourdieu, P. and M. Mammeri [1978] (2004) 'Dialogue sur la poésie orale en
Kabylie', *Actes de la recherche en sciences sociales* 23, 51–66.

—— (2004) [1978] 'Dialogue on Oral Poetry', *Ethnography* 5.4, 511–51.

Bourdieu, P. and J.-C. Passeron [1964] (1979) *Les héritiers: Les étudiants et la culture*, Paris: Éditions de Minuit.

—— [1970] (1977) *La reproduction: Éléments pour une théorie du système d'enseignement*, Paris: Éditions de Minuit.

—— (1977) [1970] *Reproduction in Education, Society and Culture*, translated by R. Nice, London: Sage.

—— (1979) [1964] *The Inheritors: French Students and their Relations to Culture*, translated by R. Nice, Chicago: University of Chicago Press.

Bourdieu, P. and M. de Saint-Martin [1976] 'Anatomie du goût', *Actes de la recherche en sciences sociales* 2.5, 5–81.

Bourdieu, P. and A. Sayad [1964] *Le déracinement: La crise de l'agriculture traditionnelle en Algérie*, Paris: Éditions de Minuit.

Bourdieu, P. and L. J. D. Wacquant (1992a) [1992b] *An Invitation to Reflexive Sociology*, Chicago: University of Chicago Press.

—— [1992b] (1992a) *Réponses: Pour une anthropologie réflexive*, Paris: Éditions du Seuil.

Texts and digital media by other authors

Bachelard, G. (1994) *The Poetics of Space,* Boston, MA: Beacon Press.

—— (2006) *The Formation of the Scientific Mind*, Manchester: Clineman Press.

Barthes, R. (1990) *The Fashion System*, translated by M. Ward and R. Howard, Berkeley, CA: University of California Press.

Becker, H. (1982) *Art Words*, Berkeley, CA: University of California Press.

Bennett, T., M. Emmison and J. Frow (1999) *Accounting for Taste: Aesthetics of Everyday Cultures*, Cambridge, UK: Cambridge University Press.

Bennett, T., M. Savage, E. Silva, A. Warde, M. Gayo-Cal and D. Wright (2009) *Culture, Class, Distinction*, London and New York: Routledge.

Bocock, R. (1995) *Consumption*, London: Routledge.

Carles, P. (director), A. Gonzalez and V. Frégosi (producers) [2001] (2002) *Sociologie est un sport combat* [DVD], Paris: Icarus Films.

—— (2002) [2001] *Sociology Is a Martial Art* [DVD], Paris: Icarus Films.

Certeau, M. de (1984) *The Practice of Everyday Life*, translated by S. Rendell, Berkeley, CA: University of California Press.

Davis, M. (1996) *Planet of Slums*, London: Verso.

Engels, F. (2009) *The Condition of the Working Class in England,* Harmondsworth: Penguin.

Fiske, J. (1991) *Understanding Popular Culture*, London: Routledge.

Foucault, M. (1991) *Discipline and Punish: The Birth of the Prison,* translated by A. Sheridan, Harmondsworth: Penguin.

—— (2003) *The Birth of the Clinic*, 3rd edn, translated by A. Sheridan, London: Routledge.

Fowler, B. (1994) 'The Hegemonic Work of Art in the Age of Electronic Reproduction: An Assessment of Pierre Bourdieu', *Theory, Culture & Society* 11.1, 129–54.

—— (1997) *Pierre Bourdieu and Cultural Theory: Critical Investigations*, London, Newbury Park, CA and New Delhi: Sage.

—— (1999) 'Pierre Bourdieu's Sociological Theory of Culture', *Variant* 8, Summer, 1–4.

Frow, J. (1987) 'Accounting for Tastes: Some Problems in Bourdieu's Sociology of Culture', *Cultural Studies* 1.1, 59–73.

—— (1995) *Cultural Studies and Cultural Value*, Oxford: Clarendon Press.

Garnham, N. and R. Williams (1980) 'Pierre Bourdieu and the Sociology of Culture: An Introduction', *Media, Culture & Society* 2, 209–23.

Goodman, J. E. (2003) 'The Proverbial Bourdieu: Habitus and the Politics of Representation in the Ethnography of the Kabylia', *American Anthropologist* 105.4, 782–93.

Goodman, J. E. and P. A. Silverstein (eds) (2009) *Bourdieu in Algeria: Colonial Politics, Ethnographic Practices, Theoretical Developments*, Lincoln: Nebraska University Press.

Grenfell, M. (2004) *Pierre Bourdieu: Agent Provocateur*, London, New York: Continuum.

Grenfell, M. and C. Hardy (2007) *Art Rules: Pierre Bourdieu and the Visual Arts*, Oxford: Berg.

Hanks, W. F. (2005) 'Pierre Bourdieu and the Practices of Language', *Annual Review of Anthropology* 34, October, 67–83.

Hesmondhalgh, D. (2006) 'Bourdieu, the Media and Cultural Production', *Media, Culture & Society* 28.2, 211–31.

Hillier, J. and E. Rookesby (eds) (2005) *Habitus: A Sense of Place,* Aldershot: Ashgate.

Holsinger, B. (2005) *The Premodern Condition: Medievalism and the Making of Theory*, Chicago: University of Chicago Press.

Honneth, A. (1986) 'The Fragmented World of Symbolic Forms: Reflections on Pierre Bourdieu's Sociology of Culture', *Theory, Culture & Society* 3.3, 55–66.

Jenkins, R. (2002) *Pierre Bourdieu*, London: Routledge.

Kuhn, T (1962) *The Structure of Scientific Revolutions*, Chicago: Chicago University Press.

Lefebvre, H. (1991) *The Social Production of Space*, translated by D. Nicholson-Smith, Maldon, MA, Oxford and Carlton, Victoria: Editions Anthropos.

Lévi-Strauss, C. (1983) *The Raw and the Cooked*, Chicago: Chicago University Press.

L'Hôte, Gilles (director) [1996] *Le champ journalistique et la télévision* [VHS video (SECAM)], Paris: Collège de France/CNRS Audiovisuel/Arts et éducation. Shown first on French television in 1996 as two one-hour programmes and subsequently released in VHS video format.

Lipstadt, H. (2000) 'Theorising Competitions', *Thresholds* 21, Fall, 32–6.

—— (2001) 'Learning from St Louis', *Harvard Design Magazine* 14, Summer, 4–15.

—— (2003) 'Can "art Professions" Be Bourdieuean Fields of Cultural Production?: The Case of the Architecture Competition', *Cultural Studies* 17.3–4, 390–419.

—— (2004) 'Pierre Bourdieu: Images d'Algérie', *Journal of the Society of Architectural Historians* 63.1, 104–6.

Löfgrem, O. (2003) 'The Sweetness of Home: Class, Culture and Family Life in Sweden', in S. M. Low and D. Lawrence-Zúñiga (eds), *The Anthropology of Space and Place: Locating Culture*, Oxford: Blackwell Publishing, pp. 142–59.

Lury, C. (1999) *Consumer Culture*, Cambridge, UK: Polity.

Mann, D. A. (1980) 'Architecture, Aesthetics and Pluralism: Theories of Taste as a Determinant of Architectural Standards', *Journal of Popular Culture* 13.4, 701–19.

McRobbie, A. (1998) *British Fashion Design*, London: Routledge.

Mitchell, T. (1988) *Colonizing Egypt*, Berkeley, CA: University of California Press.

a Determinant of Architectural Standards', *Journal of Popular Culture* 13.4, 701–19.

McRobbie, A. (1998) *British Fashion Design*, London: Routledge.

Mitchell, T. (1988) *Colonizing Egypt*, Berkeley, CA: University of California Press.

Panofsky, E. (1939) *Studies in Iconology: Humanistic Themes in the Art of the Renaissance*, New York: Oxford University Press.

—— (1951) *Gothic Architecture and Scholasticism,* Latrobe, PA: Archabbey Press.

—— (1955) *Meaning in the Visual Arts*: *Papers In and On Art History*, Garden City, NY: Doubleday.

Pellow, D. (2004) 'The Architecture of Female Seclusion in West Africa', in S. M. Low and D. Lawrence-Zúñiga (eds), *The Anthropology of Place and Space*, Oxford: Blackwell Publishing, pp. 160–83.

Prior, N. (2005) 'A Question of Perception: Bourdieu, Art and the Postmodern', *British Journal of Sociology* 56.1, 123–39.

Robben, A. C. G. M. (1989) 'Habits of the Home: Spatial Hegemony and the Structuration of House and Society in Brazil', *American Anthropologist* 91.3, 570–88.

Robbins, D. (1991) *The Work of Pierre Bourdieu: Recognising Society*, Milton Keynes: Open University Press.

—— (ed.) (2000a) *Bourdieu and Culture*, London: Sage.

—— (ed.) (2000b) *Pierre Bourdieu*, 4 vols, London: Sage.

—— (ed.) (2005) *Pierre Bourdieu 2*, 4 vols, London: Sage.

Rocamora, A. (2002a) 'Fields of Fashion: Critical Insights into Bourdieu's Sociology of Culture', *Journal of Consumer Culture* 2.3, 341–62.

—— (2002b) '*Le Monde*'s *discours de mode*: Creating the *créateurs*', *French Cultural Studies* 13, 83–98.

Sartre, J.-P. (1991) *The Family Idiot: Gustave Flaubert, 1821–1857*, 5 vols, translated by C. Cosman, Chicago: University of Chicago Press.

Savage, D. (director) (2009) *Freefall* [television programme], BBC2, London, 14 July.

Schücking, L. L. (1998) *The Sociology of Literary Taste*, London: Routledge.

Schultheis, F. (2007) 'Pictures from Algeria', *Sociology Magazine*, March, 22–8.

Silverstein, P. A. (2004) 'Of Rooting and Uprooting', *Ethnography* 5.4, 553–7.

Slater, D. (1997) *Consumer Culture and Modernity*, London: Polity.

Stevens, G. (2002) *The Favoured Circle: The Social Foundations of Architectural Distinction*, Cambridge, MA: MIT Press.

Swartz, D. L. (1997) *Culture and Power: The Sociology of Pierre Bourdieu*, Chicago: University of Chicago Press.

Swartz, D. L. and V. L. Zolberg (eds) (2005) *After Bourdieu: Influence, Critique, Elaboration*, Dordrecht, Boston, MA and London: Kluwer Academic Publishers.

Varnelis, K. (1998) 'Education of the Innocent Eye', *Journal of Architectural Education* 51.4, 212–23.

Wacquant, L. (2004) 'Following Pierre Bourdieu into the Field', *Ethnography* 5.4, 387–414.

Weber, M. (2001) *The Protestant Ethic and the Spirit of Capitalism*, translated by T. Parsons, London and New York: Routledge.

Williams, R. (1981) *Culture*, London: Fontana.

Yacine, T. (2004) 'Pierre Bourdieu in Algeria at War: Notes on the Birth of Engaged Ethno-sociology', *Ethnography* 5.4, 487–509.

Websites

Hyper Bourdieu World Catalogue is a comprehensive bibliography and mediagraphy of all works and public statements by Pierre Bourdieu. Available online at: http://hyperbourdieu.jku.at/hyperbourdieustart.html.

Index

habitus: aesthetic perception 99;
cultural production 68, 78; ethos
comparison 62; Flaubert 94; Gothic
architecture and scholasticism link
70–2; Panofsky's influence on
Bourdieu 68–9, 70–1; reproduction
via education 75; theory of practice
44, 73; unconscious processes 68
Hanks, William 70
'Haute couture et haute culture' 81,
82, 83
Les héritiers: les étudiants et la culture
6, 32, 38, 41
Hesmondhalgh, David 96
high culture 32, 34–5, 41, 54, 83
Hillier, Jean 108
Holsinger, Bruce 69, 71
Homo academicus 8
housing 54–5; Algeria 16; field of
production 86–91; house builders
88–9; Kabyle house 21, 22–9, 30
Husserl, Edmund 11
Hyper Bourdieu World Catalogue 108

inequalities 32–3, 41, 51, 57, 81, 101
'intellectual collective' 105, 106
intellectuals 52, 74–5, 100, 103, 105
International Parliament of Writers
105–6
'L'invention de la vie d'artiste' 93, 94

Jenkins, Richard 29
'Un jeu chinois' 52

Kabyle 10, 17, 18, 21, 22–9, 30–1
Kant, Immanuel 51

knowledge 36–7
Kuhn, Thomas 72

Lefebvre, Henri 16–17
legitimacy 63, 77, 78
Lévi-Strauss, Claude 5, 11, 20, 21–2
Liber (journal) 8, 105
Libre-Échange 103–4
Lipstadt, Hélène 56, 108
literary field 92, 100

'La maison kabyle ou le monde
renversé' 22–4
Mâle, Émile 69
Manet, Édouard 102, 106
Mann, Dennis 56
'Le marché des biens symboliques'
42–3, 52, 75, 78, 96
Marichal, Robert 71
Marx, Karl 12, 20
Marxism 7, 20
media 9, 54, 100, 103, 104
Méditations pascaliennes 8
*Le métier de sociologue: Préalables
épistémologiques* 33, 58, 74
middle class 45, 51; *see also*
bourgeoisie; petit bourgeoisie
migrants 14–15, 16
La misère du monde 9, 103
modernism 105
museums 33–5

nature-culture binary opposition 28
neo-liberalism 3, 8–9, 54, 91, 100,
101, 102–5, 106